A PRETTY WRECK

From Trauma to Triumph

a memoir by

Prophetess Leah M. Kelley

BLUE FORGE PRESS
Port Orchard ✵ Washington

For information about film, reprint or other subsidiary rights, contact: blueforgegroup@gmail.com

This book is a memoir. It reflects the authors' present recollections of experiences over time. While all the stories in this book are true as the author remembers them, some names and identifying details may have been changed to protect the privacy of the people involved.

Blue Forge Press is the print division of the volunteer-run, federal 501(c)3 nonprofit, Blue Legacy (EIN 83-4307421), founded in 1989 and dedicated to supporting artisans marginalized due to race, age, disability, economics or other factors. We strive to empower storytellers from all walks of life with our four divisions: Blue Forge Press, Blue Forge Films, Blue Forge Gaming, and Blue Forge Sound. Find out more at www.BlueForgeGroup.org

Blue Forge Press
7419 Ebbert Drive Southeast
Port Orchard, Washington 98367
blueforgepress@gmail.com

To my Lord and Savior, Jesus Christ —
The head of my life.
Without you, I never would have made it.
You carried me through every storm,
and I give You all the glory.

In loving memory of my precious daughter,
Adrienne C.E. Green—
Forever in my heart. Never out of mind.
Rest in peace, baby girl.

And to my now-adult children —
We made it by God's grace.
Love you all, always and forever.

Table of Contents

Forward

*I*t is with great excitement and honor that I introduce to you this incredible book, *A Pretty Wreck: From Trauma To Triumph*. The author, Leah M. Kelley, has an extraordinary story to share with the world, and I am confident that it will leave an indelible impression on you, just as it did on me.

I had the privilege of meeting Leah over a year ago when she was cast as Diamond in the upcoming movie project, *Shattered Diamond*. Little did I know then that her life story would be so compelling, so inspiring, that it would leave me at the edge of my seat as I read through the pages of her book.

The title of the book, *A Pretty Wreck: From Trauma to Triumph*, is a perfect representation of Leah's journey through life. She has encountered obstacles and challenges that would have broken most people, but she has persevered through them all with tenacity and strength that is truly remarkable. Her message, her story, is one of reclaiming power and overcoming adversity, and it is a message that we all need to hear.

As you delve into these pages, I urge you to keep an open mind and allow yourself to be moved by Leah's words. I guarantee that her story will leave a lasting impact on you, and you will find yourself hungry for more of her powerful message.

I am privileged to have been given the opportunity to share Leah's story with you, and I am confident that you will find it to be an impeccable masterpiece that is both heartwarming and thought-provoking.

Sincerely,
Larry Slack, *Actor*

Introduction

I wasn't supposed to survive—at least that's what life tried to convince me.

I was conceived in violence, born into a war zone of shame, silence, and survival. Raised in a house full of secrets, I learned early how to fake a smile and cover up bruises—some visible, most not. From the womb, my presence was unwanted, yet somehow divinely preserved. My life has never been simple, but it has always been significant.

This is not just a story of trauma. It's a story of triumph over what tried to bury me.

I am the daughter of a teenage mother, a survivor of generational dysfunction, domestic violence, kidnapping, betrayal, heartbreak, and disappointment. I have lived through abandonment, endured abuse, wiped tears in silence, and prayed for strength when my legs could barely stand.

And yet—here I am. Still standing. Still healing. Still becoming.

This memoir is not written from a place of pity, but purpose. I am a pretty wreck: broken but beautiful, damaged but delivered, wounded but walking in victory. If you've ever felt like life handed you more than you could bear, I pray these pages remind you that you are not alone—and that your story isn't over.

Welcome to my truth. It's raw. It's real. But it's mine.

Prophetess Leah M. Kelley

A PRETTY WRECK

From Trauma to Triumph

a memoir by

Prophetess Leah M. Kelley

Chapter 1

Inheritance

My mom was raised in a Christian home, with values that were deeply embedded in her from a young age. Faith was woven into the fabric of her life, and though her journey with it was personal and sometimes complex, those Christian roots were a constant foundation. There was a spiritual tug or war that raged within the confines of those walls. A war that was not visible to the outside world. An entity that opposed the very foundation of those beliefs. My grandfather would invite witches into the home, they would have seances, and speak over the children. Doors were opened. The enemy of our souls then had access. The thief cometh not but to steal, kill, and to destroy. For us to understand where the generational trauma began we must always go back to its origin. I thank God for my grandmother who stood on the front lines and served notice to the devil that he could not have her family. The schemer, the deceiver, plotted individually how he would attack them all. Isaiah 54:17 says, *"No weapon that is formed against thee shall prosper; and every tongue that shall rise against thee in judgment thou shalt condemn. This is the heritage of the servants of the Lord, and their righteousness is of me, saith the Lord."* The spirit of rebellion, and disobedience had attached itself to my mother. She would often leave home for various reasons, ending up in places, and in the company of those who meant absolutely no good. My mother was one of the prettiest of my grandmother's daughters.

She had a medium build, and her presence was commanding, with an energy that could light up a room even in the quiet moments. Her hair as I remembered was a beautiful, soft-coarse texture, worn in a natural afro that framed her face perfectly. I remember the way her hair felt when she leaned down close enough for me to touch it—it had a bit of spring, a kind of natural strength and softness that felt uniquely hers. Allow me to set the stage and give you a little background of where she grew up.

She grew up in Stamford, Connecticut, raised in a home filled with secrets. My grandparents, Robert Ford Kelley and Erma Jean Kelley, raised her with eight siblings in a house on Pressprich Street. Their home had its own things that were taboo to even mention. Shaped by the Southern roots of my grandparents who brought pieces of that world to Connecticut. There was laughter, tears, pain, life was not always easy. Her mother, my grandmother, would sometimes bring home Kentucky Fried Chicken after a long day at work, and this small gesture became a favorite treat, a taste of comfort that my mom carried with her. My mom conveyed this was one of her childhood memories. I wanted to get close to my mother so I began to ask the questions I believed would forge a closer bond.

I knew her favorite color was green—all shades of it. Green seemed to represent a part of her that connected to nature, growth, and vitality. She had a soft spot for the soulful music of Aretha Franklin, and *Respect* was more than just a song to her. It resonated with a part of her that valued dignity and self-worth, qualities she held onto even when life became challenging. She loved Southern cooking, especially when it was prepared by her mother. Collard greens, pasta, salads, and that fried chicken were her favorites, each dish carrying memories and flavors that reminded her of her family. Family was important, valued, and loved. And, yet family oftentimes can become your worst enemies. She lived in a home where if only the walls could talk was a reality. I'm not saying every day was a nightmare, but what I am saying in the lives of her siblings decades later wounds still remain, where healing should have been allowed to take place.

Where dysfunction goes unhealed, it becomes an incubator for generational incapacity, passing down broken patterns instead of breaking them.

My mother was only sixteen or seventeen when her world was shattered by a group of strangers—a trauma inflicted upon her by a gang of faceless aggressors who emerged out of nowhere and forever altered the course of her life. They gang raped my mother, the assault was unexpected, a horrifying moment that came without warning, and though she never disclosed the exact location or the details of that day, the impact was unmistakable and everlasting. I asked her if she knew, or could she identify her assailants, and her response to me was a stern *No.*

Some wounds are simply too raw, too painful to voice, and she carried this trauma as a silent burden, protecting it from the light of day. She couldn't bear to relive the horror by describing every agonizing second, so the specifics remained a closely guarded secret. In time, I came to understand that there are moments in life that refuse to be put into words—moments that continue to echo in your soul, echoing in silence, reverberating in the shadows of your memory. My mother bore the weight of her ordeal with unimaginable courage, but beneath the surface, I could always sense the hidden scars. There was something she held concealed in the corridors of her mind, that only she and God knew.

The men who assaulted her were complete strangers, and in that cruel, senseless act of violence, they stole a part of her innocence and altered her destiny forever. She didn't know their names, didn't have any connections to them—only the searing memory of their cruelty remained. They were shadows, nameless figures in her nightmares, and their existence in her life was brief yet devastating. For years, I tried to comprehend the magnitude of the pain she must have endured, the fear and isolation she must have felt as she realized what had happened to her.

Discovering she was pregnant with me only compounded her heartbreak and confusion. At a time when she should have been worrying about school dances or dreaming of the future, she was instead grappling with an unthinkable reality. Her body and soul were marred by trauma, and now she was faced with a pregnancy that was a constant reminder of the violence she had endured. Telling her parents was one of the hardest things she ever had to do, a moment that carried the weight of fear, shame, and the fragile hope for understanding and support.

I often wonder about the emotional landscape of that conversation, the tension in the air, and the expressions on my grandparents' faces when they first heard the news. Though I can't recount the exact words exchanged or how they processed this devastating revelation, I imagine it must have been met with a complex mix of disbelief, horror, grief, and anger. They were loving parents, but in that moment, their world, too, was shattered. The news that their teenage daughter had been violated and was now carrying a child must have felt like an insurmountable blow, an unraveling of the future they had envisioned for her.

The emotional toll of that moment can't be overstated. My mother's pain was like an unhealed wound, raw and festering beneath the surface, and she was left grappling with a reality she never wanted or imagined. Her dreams were stripped away, and she was thrust into adulthood prematurely, all because of a horrific act of violence. The anguish she felt was suffocating, compounded by the societal pressures and stigma that often accompany these situations. Her pregnancy, far from being a moment of joy, was steeped in feelings of shame and confusion. She carried me in a womb that bore the trauma of violence, and she faced the monumental task of deciding what to do next.

In those days, conversations around pregnancy resulting from assault were even more hushed than they are now. Women were often judged harshly, with little regard for the circumstances that led to their pregnancies. My mother considered not keeping me, a choice that weighed heavily on her heart. It wasn't a decision made lightly, but rather a contemplation born out of a desperate desire to find some semblance of peace, to erase the hurt and start over. She thought about abortion, an option that was whispered about, she wanted so desperately a life unburdened by the trauma she was carrying.

But despite the weight of these considerations, she chose to carry me to term. It was a choice marked by pain, but also a testament to her strength. My mother was wounded, deeply and irrevocably, yet she found a way to endure. There was no playbook for how to navigate such a complicated and heart-wrenching experience, yet she pressed on, even when the world felt impossibly heavy. I've often marveled at the strength it must have taken to wake up every day, to face the world with her head held high, even when she felt broken beyond repair.

When she finally told me about her assault and

the circumstances of my conception, it was a revelation that changed my understanding of my very existence. It didn't come easily; it took years of my gentle probing, years of me sensing there was something unspoken between us. When she finally shared the truth, I could hear the echoes of her pain, reverberating through the years. Her voice trembled, carrying the weight of an agony that time had not erased. I remember feeling a profound sense of disbelief, like the ground had been pulled out from under me. It was as if the foundation of my understanding of who I was had cracked, and I was left to piece together a new narrative—one that was steeped in trauma but also in resilience.

The idea that my life had begun in such devastating circumstances was difficult to process. It made me feel as though my very existence was a paradox—a source of both pain and love.

I carry the blood of my mother's rapist in my veins. The man who fathered me was a man of violence, his name unknown, but his legacy unmistakable. I didn't ask for his DNA, but I had to make a choice: to let his violence define me or to let God refine me. Forgiveness wasn't for him, it was for me. Because carrying his blood didn't mean I had to carry his curse.

I struggled to reconcile the horror of what my mother endured with the love she poured into me. Yet, as I grappled with this complex truth, I also became acutely aware of the strength it must have taken for her to raise me. Despite the trauma that marked my conception, my mother loved me fiercely, and she fought every day to give me a life that was filled with hope, not despair.

Her journey was far from easy. The weight of her trauma didn't simply dissipate after I was born; it lingered, an invisible burden she carried in her heart and mind. The scars of that violence shaped her in ways that I may never fully understand, but they also revealed a depth of resilience that I deeply admire. She was a warrior in her own right, battling demons that were never of her choosing but ones she had no choice but to confront. One thing I can say is her faith in God remained the same.

As a young child, I felt a mix of admiration and confusion toward my mom. She was a figure of strength, but also one who could feel distant at times. She would tell us growing up she never wanted any children at all, although she had 7 of us. Three she kept and four 2 sets of twins she gave up for adoption. My mothers hand was forced in that situation, yet another mental trauma to endure.

There were moments I wanted more closeness, a sense of security that I couldn't always find. She was in and out of my life, and I spent a significant part of my childhood with my grandmother, surrounded by a different rhythm of care and attention. The streets also played a role in raising me, adding layers to my understanding of family and survival that weren't typical for most children. This complicated my feelings toward her as a teenager; I longed for her presence but also grew accustomed to her absences, and it shaped my sense of independence. Growing up, I truly believed she loved us. I believe the tools to bring about, and execute the life she truly wanted for us were not available, or tangible.

When a child isn't taught right or given the tools to thrive, they grow into adults still searching. And when they have children of their own,

From Trauma to Triumph

that absence echoes, causing the next generation

to suffer in one way or another.

Now, as an adult, my feelings toward her have deepened with understanding. I am no longer bitter, I no longer harbor unforgiveness inside my heart. I understand it was hard real hard for her. And, without the help from the almighty God, neither of us would have made it.

I love and respect her for who she is, both for the things she was able to give and for the things she couldn't. I honor her resilience, her humanity, and the unique qualities she brought into my life. Her determination fueled her ambitions. Defeat was not an option.

From my mother, I inherited a love for the arts,

writing poetry, collecting antiques, and seeing beauty

others overlook. For that, I am truly grateful.

The past is part of our story, but it doesn't define my love for her now. I see her as a whole person, someone who faced her own struggles and did the best she could within her circumstances.

The memory of my mother from when I was five years old is rooted deeply, but still feels fragmented. We were living in the projects of Stamford, Connecticut. I remember the emptiness of our apartment—it felt bare, like a hollow space with walls stripped of any warmth or personality. No family photos graced the walls, no pictures, no softening touches anywhere to make it feel like a real home. It was a stark environment, almost as if any sense of family connection was absent, just a space with minimal furniture to occupy it.

That day, I remember my mother standing in the doorway, her face a mix of something I couldn't fully understand then—perhaps worry or something even heavier. Her voice was firm, instructing me not to open the door for anyone while she was away. She was leaving, and I was left to care for my two younger siblings. I was only five, yet there I was, being handed responsibility far beyond my years.

No scent stands out in my memory of that moment—no smells of food or flowers, just a blank, slightly stale smell of the apartment, like the air was as unremarkable as the rest of the room. Even now, I strained to remember whether there was anything unique about the atmosphere, but it just felt empty.

I couldn't tell you if it was winter, spring, or fall. The temperature doesn't come to mind, which only adds to my sense of detachment. I think it's as if the room was suspended in a neutral zone, not warm, not cold—just *there*. I was detached from everything around me, focusing solely on what I had been told to do: stay inside and watch over my siblings.

The overwhelming feeling was one of abandonment. It's strange to look back and see how much I shouldered emotionally for a child of five. There was a weight to that responsibility, a feeling that I had to become someone who could protect and care for others, even when I was so small myself. I don't remember what I was wearing that day. The physical details of my own self—my clothes, my hair, the feel of the fabric on my skin—are absent. It's like I disappeared from the memory altogether. I didn't yet know what it felt like to receive affection from my mother. There were no kisses or words of comfort. Not to say that she didn't love me, but at that age, I hadn't yet experienced the gestures that would have conveyed that love. Her words were clear, her instructions given with no softness, just an expectation for me to comply.

There was something about that moment that stirred an instinct in me to protect. I felt a seriousness I couldn't explain, but it felt like my whole body was in a state of high alert. I think of myself sitting in the apartment, the stillness thickening around me. I would watch the door, listen for sounds in the hallway, and occasionally peeking to check on my younger siblings. There was an inner monologue running through my head, a kind of silent promise that I wouldn't let anything bad happen to them.

There was an old television, black and white, positioned in the living room, and the grainy image flickered softly, playing my favorite show. That little screen seemed to hold a kind of allure for me, a doorway to somewhere far more colorful than the world around me.

I recall how I loved watching *Police Woman*. There was something about that show that gave me a sense of power or control—something I certainly lacked in real life. Watching the characters on TV handle danger and take control of difficult situations might have been my own way of imagining that I, too, could protect those I loved.

Touching anything in that apartment gave a sense of its age. The furniture, worn with time, felt rough and cold. When I would press my hand against the walls, they felt hard and unyielding, adding to the feeling of starkness. My feet, bare against the cool linoleum floor, could feel every groove, every chill radiating from below. It was as if the floor itself was absorbing all the warmth and life around it.

The air in the apartment held a stillness that felt heavy, like the apartment hadn't been aired out in a while. It wasn't a smell I can define, but more of an absence—and absence of warmth, of home. I suppose you could call it stale, a kind of flat, closed-off atmosphere that seemed to linger in the corners of each room. There wasn't any comforting aroma from cooking or the scent of a familiar perfume; just a quiet emptiness.

I've never returned to Stamford, Connecticut, or to that apartment where my first memories unfolded. Our family moved to Milwaukee, Wisconsin, and since then, life has led me away from Stamford. For a while, though, I held a longing to return, almost as if visiting could answer some questions or unlock memories that have stayed just out of reach. I wanted to see where it all began, to stand on the ground that first shaped me and to somehow connect with that place of my origin. But I recently learned that the complex has since been demolished. The place that held my earliest memories no longer exists, at least not in a physical sense.

In some ways, knowing it's gone gives me a

bittersweet sense of closure. It's like the place has become a memory, much like the experiences I have of it. There's nothing tangible to return to, only images and feelings that live within me. Perhaps that's how it's meant to be, that I should carry those memories inside rather than in a place I could revisit.

Over the years, my relationship with my mother has transformed profoundly. Where bitterness and confusion once filled the gaps between us, love and forgiveness have found their place, a blessing I can only attribute to the grace of the Almighty God. As a child and even a teenager, I struggled with feelings of resentment and longing—for the attention, the closeness, and the sense of security that I didn't feel growing up. But through growth and faith, our relationship has softened, evolved into something healthy, and, most importantly, something real. This love I share with my mother now is a gift I once thought was out of reach, something I deeply desired from my youth but wasn't sure would ever fully blossom.

I feel grateful beyond words for how far we've come. There's a peace in this new dynamic that I treasure, a feeling of completeness that wasn't there before. We now share a bond filled with respect, understanding, and genuine love—a relationship I'm so thankful to have, especially knowing how differently it could have turned out.

Throughout my life, I have wondered how differently things might have been if my mother's assault had never happened. I've pondered the dreams she had before her world was turned upside down, the life she could have lived if not for the violence inflicted upon her. Yet, I also recognize that her strength, her perseverance, and her love have shaped me into who I am. I carry her story with me, not as a source of shame but as a testament to the strength that runs in my veins. Her pain, while unspeakable, has also been a catalyst for the legacy of love and resilience she has passed down to me.

There were many moments in my life where I wished things had been different, where I wished for a sense of normalcy, a childhood unmarked by fear and pain. But as I grew, I began to understand the complexity of my mother's love, the ways she fought for us, even if those ways were flawed. Her strength, even when born out of brokenness, was something I came to respect deeply. She had given us everything she had, even when she had very little left to give.

The curse of trauma and abuse that plagued our family was not something that could be easily broken. It was a cycle, a pattern of pain that needed intentional healing and time to unravel. But I knew that acknowledging it, naming it, and speaking about it was the first step toward healing. My mother's story and mine are intertwined, but they are also stories of survival. We are more than what happened to us; we are more than the pain we endured.

If my mother were standing in front of me today, I would want her to know that I see her. I see her struggles, her strength, her moments of vulnerability, and the love that she gave us despite everything. I would tell her: *"Mom, I understand now. I see your pain, and I honor your strength. You faced unimaginable nightmares and still tried to give me a life filled with love. Thank you for surviving, for fighting, and for loving me the best way you knew how. And, most of all, thanks for allowing God to take the helm of your life. Thanks for allowing God to heal every wound, put the pieces back together. No longer broken, whole lacking nothing."*

"If the Son therefore shall make you free, ye shall be free indeed."

John 8:36 (KJV)

Chapter 2

Roots

Family forms the bedrock of who we are. It is where we first learn to love, adapt, and grow. My relationship with my younger family members has been a journey of deep connection, challenges, and shared perseverance. While I wouldn't call our family bonds dysfunctional, we faced obstacles, often rooted in the unstable environments around us. These challenges tested us, shaped our individual journeys, and ultimately strengthened the love that ties us together.

Growing up, our surroundings didn't always nurture our well-being. We navigated spaces filled with uncertainty and lacked the consistent guidance that children often need. Yet, through it all, we leaned on one another, turning moments of adversity into opportunities to grow stronger together.

One of the most difficult experiences I remember happened while living in Milwaukee. My siblings, and cousins, and I were entrusted to a babysitter who, instead of protecting us, became a source of harm.

She tried to make us touch each other in ways that were not right introducing confusion, shame, and brokenness far too early. Even the use of furniture was twisted into something inappropriate. These were dark and damaging moments, but by God's grace, I survived them. And now, I speak about them—not for pity, but for freedom. For myself, and for others still living in silence. One thing I learned the hard way is we must pay close attention, and seriously vet the people we leave our children with.

This person, small in stature but severely troubled, created deep emotional wounds. I still vividly recall one desperate moment when I ran out of the house, completely exposed, naked as a jaybird in an attempt to find help from a neighbor. Though young, I understood the danger we were in and acted out of a fierce need to protect my family. My cries for help were ignored and counted as having no value or validity.

Over the years, my cousin and I have revisited those painful memories, grappling with the lingering impact they left on us. Despite the weight of those experiences, the person responsible was never held accountable, and justice eluded us. Yet, through our conversations, we have found a shared strength that continues to guide us toward healing.

Even in these difficult times, our love for one another helped us endure. We found ways to rise above the dysfunction surrounding us, forging bonds that would carry us through other challenges in life. My cousin and I were like sister cousins growing up. She had no sisters, just her brother.

Family life brought its fair share of disagreements, arguments, and misunderstandings. Like any group of siblings and cousins, we clashed as much as we laughed. But no matter how big the fight or how different our views became, our connection always found a way to mend. That love, deeply rooted in our shared experiences, allowed us to overcome even the most strained moments.

In Vacaville, California, we had a dog named Scruffy. Prophett, my sibling, owned him, and Scruffy brought a sense of normalcy to our days. Those small, joyful moments—whether it was a dog wagging his tail or a shared laugh during a quiet evening—reminded us that life held beauty, even amidst uncertainty. I regretfully must confess, I gave Scruffy away out of pure frustration that hurt my brother and till this day I am still apologizing. We must take heed to our actions, and the effect they have on others. That dog gave my brother something to love and in return a sense of being loved back.

Our educational experiences often mirrored our family life: moments of camaraderie, occasional disagreements, and the constant learning that life demanded. While I didn't attend school with my cousins, I did share the same schools with my two younger siblings briefly in Rancho Cordova, California. Those days were both exciting and challenging, as we navigated school life together, sharing secrets, helping one another, and occasionally getting into mischief.

I ran away while living in Rancho Cordova. I couldn't take it anymore and I fled to Arizona where my grandmother resided. My heart was broken because I had promised to take Prophett with me. In that moment of desperation, I was already being chased by the school principal, and I was trying to make a clean break. I thought if I went back for him, we both would have been caught, and my plan to leave would be a failure.

The challenges we faced extended beyond the classroom. Being left to fend for ourselves emotionally during pivotal moments in our lives became a recurring theme. Yet, we became each other's champions, finding ways to cheer one another on even when the odds seemed stacked against us. These shared experiences built a foundation of trust and solidarity that shaped our family dynamic.

I remember the time we were taking into child protective service, my siblings and I. It only happened one time but once was enough for me. Seeing my siblings behind closed iron doors, not knowing if we would see our mother again or be reunited was utter torment. She had left us with a friend of hers and went to Reno gambling. She hadn't called and we weren't that woman's responsibility—we had worn out our welcome entirely. She had no other choice but to do what she did. My mother thought she could trust her, not knowing the woman's patience had worn paper thin.

Amidst the chaos of our upbringing, I often found myself stepping into the role of the peacemaker. Whether it was calming tempers after an argument or mediating between siblings, I naturally took on the responsibility of maintaining harmony. While it was fulfilling to foster connection and understanding, it also came with its challenges. Carrying the weight of keeping the peace often left me neglecting my own emotional needs.

But like any sibling, I also had my mischievous moments. One memory stands out—convincing Prophett and Esha to help me take my mother's car without her permission. In our youthful excitement, we thought we could pull it off, but it quickly became clear we were in way over our heads. That experience not only taught us about consequences but also revealed how much we relied on one another, even in mischief. I couldn't drive a lick, they trusted me as we drove recklessly down Coloma Road.

Thank God for His Protection.

As I look back on those moments, it's clear we were all searching for something greater—a sense of hope, stability, and security in a world that often felt chaotic. Our trials, whether they came from our environment or our relationships, often left us feeling vulnerable. Yet, we persevered, driven by a strength that came from within and from the bonds we shared.

The hardships we endured taught us invaluable lessons about survival and compassion. From the dysfunction of our surroundings to the trials of growing up, we learned to find strength in one another. These moments didn't define us; they refined us, shaping us into individuals who could face life's challenges with courage and grace.

Family, for all its challenges and complexities, remains a constant source of unconditional love. My relationship with my younger family members reflects this truth. While disagreements and misunderstandings were inevitable, our love always brought us back together. That connection became our lifeline, carrying us through even the most difficult seasons.

I take pride in the role I've played within my family. Whether as a peacemaker, a confidant, or simply a sibling who shared in the laughter and tears, every moment has contributed to the story of who we are. These memories, both joyful and painful, have woven the fabric of our family's unique narrative.

Reflecting on my journey with my younger family members, I see a story of perseverance, love, and growth. The challenges we faced didn't define us; they strengthened us. Our shared experiences taught us the value of love, the power of forgiveness, and the beauty of finding hope in one another.

My family is my foundation. They inspire me to continue growing, loving, and striving for the best version of myself. No matter what life brings, the strength we've built together reminds me that we are never truly alone. Together, we can overcome anything.

Flashes of childhood memories with Prophett come and go like the flick of his lighter—a spark, then darkness. Back in Milwaukee, where we were for a short period of time, Prophett was always the one with a mischievous edge, curious and daring. I remember him with that lighter, saying with a grin, *"I'm gonna flick my Bic."* He'd found a way to entertain himself, and he held that lighter like it was some forbidden treasure.

I watched him, half-amused and half-nervous. I was the oldest, and there was a sense of responsibility that clung to me even then, yet Prophett had this way of drawing me in, making me wonder what he'd do next.

One day, he held the lighter up to the beige curtains, and in an instant, the fabric caught fire. I'll never forget the whoosh of the flames taking over, the thick, sharp smell of burning fabric filling the air. The flames climbed up, leaving black streaks against the light fabric, and the heat made the room feel both stifling and surreal. We both stared for a second, then jumped into action, hands moving frantically, trying to put out the fire before it spread. In that moment, I learned something critical about fire, about the danger in curiosity that goes a little too far. Prophett didn't seem fazed, though. He gave me a look that was both sheepish and a bit defiant, as if he wasn't fully sorry.

There was something I admired in him, though. Prophett had this spark, this ability to turn the ordinary into an adventure, even if it meant bending the rules or taking risks. I both wanted to protect him and stand back in awe of his boldness, his refusal to be restrained by caution. Sometimes, though, that boldness made me anxious. His unpredictability left me feeling that I needed to keep an eye on him, to make sure nothing got too far out of hand. It was as if he was testing the boundaries not just of what he could do, but of how far I was willing to follow him. Being with Prophett meant walking the line between excitement and fear, and he taught me early that not everything thrilling was safe.

Mi-Esha was quiet—so quiet that sometimes it was easy to overlook her in the noisy shuffle of our lives. But she had a presence, something steady and calm that balanced the rest of us, especially when things got a little too wild. While Prophett's energy was all sparks and fire, Mi-Esha was more like the steady embers, warm but contained. Even as a child, I could sense something different in her. She was watchful, as if taking everything in and storing it somewhere deep inside. She didn't need to say much; her eyes told you she was paying attention, noticing things most of us didn't.

One memory that comes back to me is the time we tried to straighten each other's hair with a hot comb. Mi-Esha was there, her small face watching closely, almost too closely. I remember the metallic scent of the comb heating up, the faint sizzle as it touched our hair, and the smell of singed strands when it got too close to the skin. Mi-Esha sat still as a statue, trusting, even though neither of us really knew what we were doing. I admired her calmness, the way she could just sit there, trusting, while the rest of us were full of nerves and laughter. That moment, and others like it, taught me that quiet strength could be just as powerful as all the noise and energy.

Mi-Esha was a fighter, though I didn't fully understand that until much later. Not just a fighter with her fists but someone who fought with an inner drive, a toughness that made her plus what she wanted or who she was becoming. Her quiet determination taught me that you didn't always need to shout or show off to be strong. Sometimes, the strength to sit still, to hold back, was even greater. I looked up to her for that, even if I didn't always understand it as a child.

At times, I found her quietness hard to read. I wondered what she was thinking, whether she felt the same mix of excitement and unease as I did about being left alone, about all the little adventures we found ourselves in. There was a part of me that wished she'd speak up more, that she'd let me into her world, but that wasn't her way. It was like she held her own secrets, even as we shared the same space. If Prophett's unpredictability made me anxious, Mi-Esha's silence left me curious, always guessing what was behind that calm exterior. My cousin who was two years younger than me but never acted like it. She had this bold, almost fierce presence that seemed to fill any room we were in together. She wasn't afraid to say what she wanted, and more often than not, she found a way to get it. In my child's mind, I saw her as a bit of a bully—someone who knew how to throw her weight around to make sure things went her way. I'd watch her with a mix of frustration and admiration, wondering how she could be so confident, so unbothered by what anyone else thought.

I have this flash of a memory: we were in the kitchen, that big kitchen that always felt like the center of everything. The beige curtains, the heavy stove, the way sounds seemed to echo off the walls. She had a way of setting the tone, like the rest of us were just waiting to see what she'd do next. She'd give orders in this firm, no-nonsense voice, her small face scrunched up with determination. Whether we were playing, plotting, or even arguing, she somehow always took control. At times, I resented it, but deep down, I admired her boldness. She seemed to understand power in a way I was just starting to notice, and it fascinated me even as it unsettled me.

One of the things I learned from her was resilience. She taught me, in her own way, that life wasn't always fair and that if you wanted something, you had to be willing to go after it, no matter the obstacles. Even as kids, she was teaching me about persistence—not always in the gentlest way, but the lesson stuck with me. I realized that part of her "bully" behavior was her way of asserting herself in a world where kids were often overlooked or brushed aside.

She wasn't about to let that happen to her, and I came to respect that strength, even if I didn't always enjoy it when I was on the receiving end of her pushiness.

There were times, though, when her intensity made me nervous. She didn't just want things; she demanded them, and she had no problem challenging anyone who stood in her way. I remember feeling that if she set her mind to something, she'd stop at nothing until she got it. There was a forcefulness about her that felt almost untamed, and I sometimes feared getting on her bad side. But despite her strong personality, she was family, and in her way, I knew she cared for all of us. Underneath her bossy exterior, there was a loyalty, a sense that even if she was hard on us, she'd still be there when it mattered.

Looking back, I see that she taught me to be assertive, to stand my ground when it mattered. She showed me that it was okay to want things, even if you had to fight for them, and that confidence wasn't something you waited for—it was something you created for yourself. Even though her boldness often clashed with my own quieter nature, her strength left a mark on me that I still carry today.

As we grew into our teenage years, one thing that stands out about her brother was his passion for music. He joined a band, and I can still picture him playing the drums, his hands moving with precision and rhythm. Watching him behind that drum set, I could see how deeply he connected with the beat, almost like he was in his own world. His love for music added a new layer to our family's dynamic—he'd bring this energy with him that was different from our childhood playfulness. It was a mature, focused kind of energy, like he'd found a part of himself in the music.

I remember the sound of the drums filling the room, the vibrations resonating through the walls and into the floors, pulsing with every beat he played. There was something Gripping about watching him, the rhythm steady and strong, a little piece of order in the otherwise chaotic teenage world we were navigating. Jason's commitment to his music showed me the value of having a passion, something that was yours and yours alone. In his quiet way, he taught me that creativity could be an anchor, a way to express yourself without needing words.

There's a part of my childhood that feels incomplete, a sense of absence that I didn't fully understand until I was older. My mother, young and overwhelmed, made the difficult decision to give up my four younger siblings for adoption. Two sets of twins— four lives that would grow up in homes different from mine, with memories and experiences I wouldn't be part of. I often wondered what it would have been like to have them there with us, to see their faces around our family table, to share in the chaos and laughter. There's an emptiness in knowing I missed out on those moments, that while I played and explored with the siblings and cousins I grew up with, four others were out there, living separate lives. It left me with a quiet longing, a feeling that part of our family story would always be left unwritten.

That guilt was never mine to bear.

Growing up, my mother's siblings were more than just family; they were an integral part of my journey. Each one of them left an indelible mark on my life, shaping my character and teaching me lessons that I carry with me to this day. Their love, wisdom, quirks, and even their challenges became threads in the tapestry of my upbringing.

Uncle Richard, one of my mother's four brothers, was a man of dignity and charisma. A former military man who later became a pastor, he was always impeccably dressed, with a sense of style that turned heads. Women admired him—some with genuine affection, others with admiration that bordered on infatuation. To me, however, he was simply Uncle Rickey a figure of strength, authority, and love.

I vividly recall one memorable incident that

earned me a well-deserved punishment. Uncle Rickey had sent me to the store to buy toilet paper. It was a simple task, but in my youthful distraction, I ended up at the laundromat kissing my childhood crush. Hours later, I returned home only to face the consequences. Uncle Rickey was not the type to let such behavior slide, and I quickly learned the importance of responsibility and focus. I received the beatdown of my life.

Despite his strictness, he loved me deeply, and I admired him for his discipline and dedication to family. His presence in my life instilled in me a respect for authority and the importance of doing things the right way.

Uncle Rickey was a lighthearted presence in my life. He owned a Great Dane, and in his mischievous humor, convinced me it was a small horse. He even had me ride its back, and while I didn't quite believe him, I loved his ability to make me laugh and see the world through a playful lens.

His joy and humor brought light to our family, and though he is no longer with us, those memories of laughter and adventure remain some of my fondest. He told me before he transitioned Elah you can't straddle the fence, a memory that lingers within me.

A PRETTY WRECK

My memories of Uncle Bobby began to take shape when our family moved to Tucson, Arizona, and lived at Menlo Park Apartments. Uncle Bobby was an ex-military man and a no-nonsense hustler. He was the kind of person who wouldn't tolerate foolishness but had a soft spot for family. His mantra was, *"he didn't want the hoe he had."* That would become one of his various signature sayings.

When I was younger, Uncle Bobby would pay me five cents to scratch his head—a small act that became a bonding ritual. As I grew older, our relationship evolved, and he became someone I could confide in. We often sat on the back porch, where he would share his wisdom in a way that felt like guidance without judgment. Those conversations are etched in my memory, and the lessons he imparted are ones I'll carry forever.

Uncle Bobby's strength inspired me, and his passing left a void that is still felt deeply. He would say girl kiss me right here on my forehead, cause one day i ain't gonna be here.

Aunt Pearl was more than an aunt; she was like a big sister to me. She was only about eight years older, which made her relatable and approachable during my childhood. She took care of me in ways that left a lasting impression—combing my hair, helping me get ready for school, and guiding me with her wisdom and care.

Her nurturing spirit and youthful energy were gifts that I treasured. Aunt Pearl's presence in my life taught me the importance of showing love through actions, and her passing was a loss I still feel to this day. Her lessons and love continue to guide me. And, the demons she fought remind me to stay armored up with the full armor of God, and to never take down for the devil.

Aunt Chandler, who didn't have children of her own, treated all her nieces and nephews as if they were her own. She had a gift for teaching social graces, from how to model to carrying oneself with elegance and confidence. Her lessons in poise and presentation gave me tools that I use to this day. She poured into me everything she knew, I am a protege of sorts.

Her generosity and care were unmatched, and her influence extended far beyond her immediate family. Aunt Chandler's impact on my life was profound, and I remain grateful for the gifts she gave me.

*U*ncle Terence, whom I affectionately call Uncle Tab, is my mother's only surviving brother and one of the closest family members to me. He has always been like a brother-uncle, someone I could turn to and rely on no matter what. We have what we call graveyard talks, meaning we will take to eternity what we discuss, i truly thank god for that safe place. We all need someone like that.

He is an actor by profession, Uncle Tab brought creativity and understanding into my life. I recall a time when I got in trouble for skipping school. Instead of a harsh punishment, he simply told me to go to bed without any questions asked. That moment reflected his approach to discipline: firm but caring.

To this day, Uncle Tab remains one of the most important people in my life, and our bond is one I cherish deeply.

*U*ncle Curtis, also known as "Earthquake Kelley," brought laughter and encouragement wherever he went. He had a unique ability to uplift others with his humor and inspire them to see their potential. He loved God, and preached until his dying day the gospel of Jesus Christ.

He made me feel valued and capable, even when life felt overwhelming. His support and encouragement left an indelible mark on my life, and his absence is deeply felt. His legacy of joy and positivity continues to influence me. I still can't believe he's gone. This one truly was different.

*A*unt Phyllis holds a special place in my heart. I often think back to the times we spent at her home on Farmington Way in Sacramento, California. I call these moments "muffin talks" because Aunt Phyllis made the most delicious muffins, and our conversations around her table were filled with love, insight, and wisdom.

She also had a small garden in her backyard, which reflected her nurturing spirit. Aunt Phyllis had a way of imparting life lessons in a gentle, memorable way, and her impact on my life is something I treasure deeply.

*M*y Aunt Cora is the definition of quiet strength. As the family's nurse, she became the person everyone could turn to in times of need. Her calm demeanor and listening ear made her someone you could trust implicitly. She was the only one of my mothers siblings who had the beauty mark of freckles.

Aunt Cora inspired me to chase my dreams and focus on achieving them, no matter the obstacles. Her encouragement and steady presence continue to motivate me to stay on course and push forward with determination.

Each of my uncles and aunts faced their own battles, and each fought hard to overcome the challenges life threw at them. Despite their imperfections, they embodied strength, resilience, and love. They showed me that it's possible to persevere through adversity while remaining deeply connected to family.

The lessons, love, and memories my mother's siblings gave me are gifts I will carry for the rest of my life. They were unique individuals, each with their own strengths and struggles, but through it all, they remained people I loved and who loved me in return.

They taught me not to give up when the going gets tough.

Though many of them are no longer with us, their impact lives on in the stories I tell, the values I hold, and the person I strive to become. Their legacy is a testament to the enduring power of family and the bonds that connect us through life's joys and challenges.

In them, I saw imperfect people navigating life

with their struggles and shortcomings, carrying the weight of their challenges and the "monkeys on their backs." Yet, I also witnessed their accomplishments, their love, and their quest for righteousness. The way they lived their lives left me both in admiration and heartbreak for the pain they endured.

They were great men and women who loved me deeply and tried their best to impart something meaningful to help me navigate this life. Among them were preachers, ex-cons, prostitutes, gangstas, actors, professionals, retired military, and even an ex-voodoo priest who professed that God delivered him from the enemy himself. He went on to preach the gospel of Jesus Christ around the world.

I loved my uncles and aunts dearly. For those who have passed on, they are profoundly missed. For those who remain, I cherish them deeply. Despite their imperfections, they were raised in a Christian home, and the seed of righteousness was deeply embedded in them—even when their lives sometimes seemed contrary to that teaching.

As they fought hidden battles

with unseen forces...

I count myself incredibly blessed to be their oldest niece and to have had the privilege of learning from their lives, both in their triumphs and their trials.

*F*amily shapes us in countless ways. It is where we first learn about love, perseverance, mistakes, and redemption. My mother's siblings were no exception, leaving a profound impact on my life through their individual journeys. Their experiences were a mix of triumphs and hardships, marked by moments of redemption and shadows of struggles, including addiction, incarceration, and spiritual transformations. These realities, though painful at times, became powerful lessons that shaped my values and choices.

As a child, I often observed these stories from the sidelines, too young to fully understand their depth but deeply affected by their outcomes. The lives of my uncles and aunts taught me valuable lessons—what to embrace and what to avoid. Their paths pushed me toward faith, trust in God, and a commitment to living a life of integrity.

Addiction and alcoholism were harsh realities that loomed over parts of my family. These struggles, though unspoken at times, were evident in their effects. I witnessed moments where addiction disrupted relationships, created instability, and brought pain to those involved. These experiences painted a vivid picture of how substances could change people I loved, turning them into versions of themselves I barely recognized. Oftentimes barbaric....

Though I didn't always understand the full weight of what I was seeing, I knew the consequences were profound. Addiction didn't just affect the person struggling—it rippled through the family, leaving scars on everyone. The unpredictability, the tension, and the cycles of hope and despair became a backdrop to my childhood memories.

What stood out most was how addiction could coexist with love. Those who struggled with substances were not defined by their struggles alone. They were still family, still people who cared deeply in their own way. Witnessing this complexity motivated me to choose a different path. I decided early on that substances would not hold power over my life. Instead, I turned to faith, using it as a foundation for strength, direction, and hope.

For some of my mother's siblings, life took them down paths that eventually led to incarceration. These experiences were difficult for our family, casting a shadow that was hard to ignore. Prison was not just a punishment; it became a space for reflection, a crossroads where choices and consequences collided.

Hearing about a family member being in jail or prison was confusing as a child. It created a sense of distance, both physical and emotional. Yet, these experiences also taught me about resilience and the possibility of change. Some of my uncles used their time in prison as an opportunity to reflect, grow, and find redemption. Their ability to rebuild their lives despite their mistakes became a powerful reminder that failure isn't final.

These stories showed me the importance of accountability and the strength it takes to rebuild. They reminded me to think carefully about my own decisions and to always seek a path that aligns with integrity and faith.

For some family members, the streets became their domain. Hustling was not just a way to make money; it was a means of survival in a world that didn't always provide other opportunities. This life, however, came with risks and costs. Though I didn't witness these activities directly, their consequences were clear—both in the stories passed down through the family and in the scars they left behind.

Hustling and pimping were part of a world that promised power and independence but often delivered pain and instability. The allure of quick money sometimes led to dangerous situations, creating cycles of hardship that were difficult to escape.

These stories were both cautionary tales and

lessons in complexity. I understood that the choices made by my family members were often driven by necessity rather than desire. This understanding deepened my empathy, but it also strengthened my resolve to build a life rooted in stability, honesty, and faith.

One of the most transformative stories in my family involved a sibling who transitioned from practicing voodoo to becoming a Pentecostal preacher. This shift was monumental, representing a journey from one spiritual path to another. While I wasn't present to witness this transformation firsthand, its impact on our family was undeniable.

For me, this story reinforced the idea that redemption is always possible. It reminded me that faith is not always a straight line; it is a journey filled with twists, turns, and moments of profound growth.

Certain topics in our family were rarely discussed openly. Addiction, incarceration, and spiritual conflicts were treated as taboo, things that were better left unsaid. Yet, these stories often spread through whispers, carried on the wings of gossip.

This undercurrent of secrecy and judgment created tension within the family. Gossip magnified the challenges, turning them into spectacles rather than opportunities for understanding and healing. As a child, I didn't always understand the weight of these stories, but I felt their impact. They created divisions, stirred up pain, and often overshadowed the love that held us together.

These experiences taught me the importance of compassion. I learned to look beyond mistakes and struggles, to see the humanity in each family member. They also showed me the danger of gossip and the importance of protecting family bonds, even in the face of difficult truths.

The challenges I witnessed within my family pushed me toward faith. Addiction, incarceration, and the complexities of survival all pointed to the fragility of life and the need for a foundation stronger than human willpower alone. For me, that foundation was God.

I chose to trust God, not just as a distant figure but as an active presence in my life. Faith became my refuge, a source of strength and guidance in navigating life's challenges. It was my way of ensuring that the struggles I saw wouldn't define my own path. Although I made my share of mistakes, toyed with rebellion, I found myself in unsavory situations.

Serving God wasn't just about avoiding the mistakes, it was about embracing a life of purpose, hope, and love. It was about striving for heaven, not out of fear, but out of a desire to live a life that honors God and uplifts those around me. I had to repent....

*L*ooking back on the lives of my mother's siblings, I see stories of both struggle and strength. Their journeys were not easy, but they were filled with moments of growth, love, and redemption. They showed me that no one is beyond hope and that even the hardest paths can lead to transformation.

Their lives taught me about forgiveness—forgiving others and forgiving myself. They reminded me of the power of grace to heal wounds and rebuild relationships. Most importantly, they showed me that love persists, even in the face of struggle.

The legacy of my mother's siblings is one of complexity and depth. It is a story of choices made, lessons learned, and love that endured through it all. Their experiences pushed me to pursue a life of faith, integrity, and compassion. It would be a journey of ups and downs, and my own trials and tribulations.

Though their struggles were difficult to witness, they also inspired me. They showed me the importance of resilience, the power of redemption, and the value of holding onto hope. Their stories are a testament to the enduring strength of family and the ability to grow, heal, and transform. Their lives, with all their complexity, have shaped me into the person I am today, and for that, I am grateful.

*F*amily is a cornerstone of who we are, and my mother's siblings played an integral role in shaping my life. Each one of them brought something unique to my journey—love, laughter, wisdom, and even lessons from their struggles. Over the years, their lives have changed, and for some, those lives have transitioned into the afterlife. Despite the pain of their absence, the impact they made on me remains eternal.

Out of the eight individuals I've spoken of, four of them—Uncle Bobby, Uncle Richard (or Rickey), Aunt Pearl, and Uncle Curtis—have passed on. Their departures left a void in my heart that only heaven could heal. Through the grace of God, I found peace, and the love they showed me continues to be a source of comfort. Their wisdom is etched into my memory, guiding me in ways that will never fade.

The loss of Uncle Bobby, Uncle Richard, Aunt Pearl, and Uncle Curtis was deeply felt. Each of them held a special place in my life, and their passing left behind an undeniable emptiness. Yet, in that emptiness, I found the grace of God to suture the wounds and restore my strength.

Uncle Bobby, with his tough exterior and deep wisdom, taught me lessons I will carry forever. Our porch conversations are memories I often revisit, and his belief in perseverance remains a guiding force.

From Trauma to Triumph

Uncle Richard, the well-dressed disciplinarian, showed me the value of structure, responsibility, and love that isn't afraid to correct. Even when he gave me tough lessons, I knew they came from a place of care.

Like a big sister, Aunt Pearl nurtured me with her youthful energy and unwavering support. Her presence in my life was one of guidance and unconditional love, and I miss her deeply.

Uncle Curtis, with his infectious laughter and uplifting words, reminded me of the power of joy and encouragement. His legacy as "Earthquake Kelley" brought inspiration not only to me but to everyone who knew him. He was worldly known as a mighty man of God, Teacher, Preacher, and Evangelist.

Though they are no longer with us, their love continues to live in my heart, and their lessons shape the person I am today.

As for the others, their lives have shifted in beautiful and meaningful ways. My Aunt Phyllis and Aunt Chandler are both retired, enjoying the seasons of life they worked so hard to reach. Aunt Phyllis, with her delicious muffins and garden talks, remains a source of warmth and cherished memories. Aunt Chandler, who taught me social graces and poise, still holds her elegant presence, a reflection of the values she imparted.

Uncle Terence, my Uncle Tab, continues to

thrive in his artistic endeavors. His acting career remains alive, and his artwork now graces galleries in Seattle, Washington—a testament to his creativity and determination. Watching him pursue his passions with such dedication is an inspiration.

Aunt Cora, my pillar of quiet strength, remains devoted to her work as a nurse. Though she's ready to retire, her commitment to helping others is a reflection of the care she's shown our family throughout the years. Her ability to combine strength with gentleness continues to inspire me to this day. She is a genuine soul, who possesses a sincere giving heart.

The loss of my uncles and Aunt Pearl has been softened by the passage of time and the grace of God. Heaven has healed the wounds their absence left in my heart, stitching the pain with memories of love, laughter, and the bonds we shared. Through their lives, I learned lessons of resilience, faith, and the enduring power of family.

Each of my mother's siblings, whether still living or transitioned, has left a legacy in my life. Their stories, struggles, and triumphs are threads in the fabric of who I am. While I miss those who have passed, I am grateful for the time we shared and the love they gave.

As life moves on, I carry with me the lessons of my family. Those who have passed remain with me in spirit, and those who are still here continue to inspire me with their lives. Their stories are reminders of the importance of faith, love, and perseverance, even in the face of life's challenges.

I would have many challenges to overcome in the years ahead.

Through the grace of God, I honor their memory by living a life that reflects the wisdom they imparted. I trust that the love they gave me, the lessons they taught, and the values they instilled will continue to guide me. Whether on this earth or in heaven, they are always a part of me, and for that, I am eternally grateful.

I didn't always do things right but eventually I got it right.

During my childhood, one of the most profound experiences was the trips my Uncle Tab would take us on to the planetarium at the University of Arizona. Those visits weren't merely excursions—they were journeys into a realm of infinite wonder and curiosity. I remember the feeling that would bubble up every time I learned we'd be going: a joyful expectation that seemed to lift me out of everyday life and transport me to a place filled with mystery, beauty, and endless questions waiting to be explored.

From the moment we'd begin preparing for the visit, a sense of excitement would rise within me. I'd think about the planetarium itself—its domed ceiling, the hushed darkness that seemed to wrap around us as we entered, and the way the room felt both vast and intimate at the same time. Each trip felt like a chance to leave the ordinary world behind, to step into a universe where stars, planets, and galaxies danced before my eyes. It was as if, for those precious hours, the boundaries of what I knew and understood expanded, stretching my mind and heart with the sheer scope of the cosmos. In those moments my mind was completely free from worry, free from pain, I felt as though I was no longer suffocating.

Before we even arrived at the planetarium, the journey itself was filled with wonder. Uncle Tab would gather us, and we'd get on the bus with a sense of anticipation that grew with every mile. The ride, though familiar, felt different on these days. I would gaze out the window, watching the desert landscape. Even then,

I sensed that the universe held so much more than what I saw in my day-to-day life, and these trips made me feel like a tiny part of something incredibly vast and mysterious.

When we finally arrived, my heart would race as we entered the building. I remember the feeling of stepping into the dim light of the planetarium lobby, surrounded by displays that hinted at the wonders awaiting us. Posters of stars, moons, and galaxies covered the walls, each one a small window into the vastness we were about to explore. It was a world that felt so much larger than myself, and yet, standing there, I felt as though I belonged to it, as if I had a role in the endless tapestry of the cosmos.

As we took our seats under the dome, I would feel a hush settle over the room. The lights would dim, and for a moment, everything was silent. Then, slowly, the stars would begin to appear on the ceiling above us. The transformation was breathtaking. The dark room would light up with thousands of tiny points, each representing a star millions of miles away. Planets would drift across the ceiling, their colors and sizes so vividly projected that it felt as if we could reach out and touch them. I'd lean back in my seat, eyes wide, utterly captivated by the universe unfolding above me.

Uncle Tab would sit beside us, pointing out

different constellations as they appeared. He would share stories about each one—the myths of Orion and the Seven Sisters, the tales of Cassiopeia and her eternal throne in the sky. He had a way of making these stories feel real, as though they were part of a larger narrative in which we all had a role. Each constellation wasn't just a pattern of stars; it was a story, a reminder of humanity's ancient connection to the night sky. Listening to him, I felt both small and significant, a single point of light in the vastness of existence, but one with purpose and meaning.

Each visit filled me with a sense of joyful expectation that was almost tangible. Knowing that we'd be seeing the stars, learning about planets, and listening to stories that had been passed down through generations stirred something within me. It was a feeling of possibility, a belief that there was so much more to the world than I could see or understand. Every trip felt like an adventure into the unknown, and that excitement carried over into the following days and weeks. I would lie awake at night, looking up at the stars through my window, wondering what stories they held and what secrets they might reveal if I looked hard enough.

Those planetarium visits left a mark on me that has lasted to this day. They taught me that the world is full of mysteries and that every answer leads to another question, another path to explore. This experience shaped how I view the world—not as a collection of known facts, but as a vast, intricate puzzle that will never be fully solved. It filled me with a desire to keep seeking, to keep learning, and to never settle for what I already know. There is always more to discover, always another layer to peel back, and that sense of wonder has become a guiding principle in my life.

As I grew older, this sense of curiosity only deepened. In school, I found myself drawn to subjects that encouraged exploration—science, history, literature—each one offering a new way to understand the world. But my love for the stars remained constant. I would always come back to the night sky, the memory of those planetarium visits reminding me of the vastness that lay beyond. The lessons I learned there— both from the stars and from Uncle Tab—taught me that knowledge is not a destination but a journey, one that I am still on today.

Today, this memory influences nearly every aspect of my life. Whenever I face a new challenge or opportunity, I approach it with the same sense of joyful expectation that I felt as a child. I know that there is always more to learn, always another layer to uncover, and that perspective gives me both humility and excitement. The world, as I see it, is a place of endless possibility, filled with secrets that are just waiting to be explored. This belief has become a cornerstone of who I am, shaping my approach to life, learning, and growth.

Chapter 3

Betrayal

During my early years in Milwaukee, life was often filled with challenges I couldn't fully understand at such a young age. My world was small yet heavy, filled with emotions that were hard to put into words. Amidst the confusion and noise, I found a quiet place of peace—the upstairs closet in our home.

This closet was simple and unassuming, a small space where the world seemed to pause. The dim light and the scent of old wood and fabric created a sanctuary of stillness, a place where I felt safe to just be. I would sit in the shadows, feeling comforted by the silence, and there, I would begin to speak to God. I didn't have the words to ask for everything I felt I needed, nor could I explain all that weighed on me. But somehow, sitting in that quiet space, I felt a closeness, an unspoken understanding, as if God was listening to every unvoiced feeling.

I don't remember specific questions or requests. What I do remember is the feeling of being heard. In the stillness, I felt a calmness, a comfort that wrapped around me like a warm blanket. Even though I was so young, those quiet conversations became my way of finding strength, of feeling that, despite the challenges, I was not alone. The closet became my refuge, a place where I could release the things I couldn't say out loud, finding solace in the quiet presence of God.

After I left Milwaukee at the age of five, life continued, and the experiences I carried from those early years moved with me. Though I was young, the comfort I found in that small closet stayed with me as I grew up elsewhere. I carried the memory of those quiet moments, the feeling that God was always close, even when life was far from peaceful.

As I grew older, life's challenges grew with me, and the urge to escape intensified. The closet was long gone, but the need for an escape remained. In my teenage years, I often sought new ways to cope with the stress and confusion that life brought. I felt the pull to run, to find anything that would ease the emotions I didn't know how to handle. At times, I acted out in ways that I later realized were destructive. I was searching for peace, for a way to deal with the weight I carried, but I didn't yet know how to find it in a way that truly healed.

Yet, through all the difficulties and choices I made, there was a quiet thread connecting me back to those early moments in the closet. Even when I felt far from peace, the memory of feeling God's presence in that quiet space reminded me that solace was possible. That small, unbreakable thread of faith kept me anchored, pulling me back each time I strayed too far.

As I matured, I reached a turning point. Running away from my problems no longer felt like a solution, and the old ways of escape only left me feeling more empty. I began to realize that I needed to approach life differently. True escape wasn't about avoiding pain; it was about finding strength within to face it head-on.

This shift didn't happen overnight, but gradually, I began to build new ways to handle adversity. I rediscovered the power of prayer, not as a way to run but as a source of strength. I began to approach challenges with the faith I had carried since those early years, facing each obstacle with a resolve that had quietly grown within me.

Prayer became a grounding force. I would sit with my Bible, letting the words guide me, reminding me of the same closeness I had felt as a child. These practices became my new sanctuary, a way to create the peace I once found in that small closet. There were still times, however, when escape wasn't an option. In these moments, I had to rely on something deeper, a strength that went beyond physical actions. I reminded myself of the unwavering belief I had felt in the closet years ago—that I wasn't alone and that God had a purpose for me, no matter how hard things seemed.

During these moments, I would repeat phrases to myself: *"I will get through this," "I am strong enough,"* and *"This challenge won't destroy me."* Each time I found myself in a seemingly impossible situation, I drew strength from my faith and the memory of that little girl who had found comfort in God's presence. She was still within me, now seasoned by experience but holding fast to that same, simple faith.

Through it all, I learned that survival wasn't always about physically escaping—it was about perseverance, an inner strength, and a faith that refused to be shaken. In every difficult moment, I could feel that small, quiet sanctuary within me, one that couldn't be taken away, no matter the circumstances. Reflecting on this journey, I see a clear path from the little girl in the closet to the woman I am today. Those early experiences of speaking to God in the quiet shadows taught me the value of inner peace and the power of faith. And as I grew, I learned that true escape isn't about leaving my problems behind—it's about finding a place of calm within myself that can withstand any storm.

Today, I stand strong, rooted in the lessons of my past. The greatest sanctuary I've found is within—a spiritual refuge built on faith, hope, and resilience. Through prayer, reflection, and a heart that holds fast to peace, I face life's challenges, not merely to survive but to grow. And with each step forward, I know that the same presence that comforted me as a child remains with me, guiding me toward strength, healing, and purpose.

Thank you, God, for saving a wretch like me.

*C*hildhood is often a collection of vivid moments, where certain experiences stand out and remain etched in memory. Though I can't recall every detail from those early years, some unforgettable experiences still come to mind—like the time I visited the zoo, my adventures at the park, and the vibrant gatherings at church. These memories are a beautiful patchwork of joy, wonder, and spiritual connection that have stayed with me over the years.

One particularly thrilling experience was a childhood field trip to the zoo in Milwaukee, where I went with my grandmother. The sights, sounds, and scents of the zoo filled my senses. I remember the earthy smell of the outdoors mixed with the distinct scents of the animal enclosures. The air echoed with the calls of exotic animals—the majestic roar of lions, the chattering of monkeys, and the melodic songs of birds flying above.

What made this trip unforgettable was an unexpected adventure: I fell into the anteater enclosure. Everything seemed to happen so quickly, yet I can still recall the feeling of surprise and fear. Standing inside the space meant for these strange creatures was both frightening and exhilarating. Thankfully, the situation was resolved quickly, but the memory remains as a reminder of life's unexpected twists and turns.

Equally joyful were the carefree days spent at the park with friends. The park was a haven of freedom, where laughter filled the open spaces, and the fresh scent of grass greeted us as we ran barefoot across the fields. The sensation of cool blades of grass tickling my feet still lingers in my memory. And I remember how we threw rocks at the hela monsters. We were scared of those lizards!

I loved soaring on the swings, pushing myself higher and higher until it felt as though I was flying. The rhythmic creak of the chains and the wind brushing against my face added to the sense of exhilaration.

Menlo Park will forever be etched in my mind.....

From that height, everything looked mesmerizing—trees swayed in the breeze, families gathered for picnics, and birds flitted gracefully across the sky. The world seemed limitless from the vantage point of those swings.

Playing games like tag with friends was always a highlight. We would run across the open fields, our laughter mingling with the songs of birds and the rustling of leaves. Even when we stumbled and fell, we got back up, brushed ourselves off, and kept playing. The park was our kingdom—a place where imagination thrived, and joy knew no bounds.

Church events also hold a special place in my heart. They were more than just religious gatherings; they were vibrant celebrations filled with warmth, music, and a deep sense of community. The sound of gospel music resonated through the building, uplifting everyone who heard it. The melodies of the choir, the powerful rhythm of the organ, and the heartfelt clapping of hands created a joyful and spiritual atmosphere.

I can still recall the aroma of freshly baked cakes and other delicious treats wafting through the air during these gatherings. The sweetness of those cakes, often shared after service, remains a cherished memory. They weren't just desserts—they symbolized fellowship and the joy of coming together as a community.

Beyond the delicious food and uplifting music, these events were filled with meaningful messages that nourished my spirit. The sermons, even as a child, left an impression on me. They spoke of faith, love, and perseverance, planting seeds of wisdom that would guide me throughout life.

The comforting routine of church gatherings, coupled with the presence of family, created a strong foundation for my understanding of faith and belonging. The sounds, scents, and tastes of those moments are forever etched in my mind—the laughter of community, the sweet aroma of cakes, the soul-stirring gospel music, and the unbreakable bonds formed during those gatherings.

Looking back on these experiences fills me with gratitude. They remind me of a time when life was simple, and joy could be found in the smallest of things. The thrill of unexpected adventures, the freedom of play, and the comfort of spiritual gatherings all contributed to shaping the person I am today.

These memories continue to inspire me to find joy in life's simple pleasures, cherish connections with others, and approach each day with a sense of wonder and gratitude. They are a testament to the beauty of childhood and the lasting impact of moments filled with love, laughter, and faith.

*L*ooking back on my childhood, my memories outside the home are few and far between. Most of my time was spent within the familiar walls of our house, where I felt safe—until that sense of security was shattered by a deceitful and manipulative act.

When I was five years old, an event occurred that shattered my sense of safety and innocence, marking the beginning of a life shaped by experiences far too heavy for a child to carry. My mother, with the weight of her own trauma heavy on her shoulders, had warned me not to open the door for anyone while she was away. Her voice had a gravity I couldn't fully comprehend at that age. I didn't yet understand the darkness that could invade even the safest spaces. I was young, naive, and trusting—a child whose only worries should have been about toys, laughter, and the wonders of the world.

But life doesn't always work in the realm of innocence. There are shadows that prey on the vulnerable, and our home, which should have been a sanctuary, became a place of fear. A neighbor—someone I recognized but didn't really know—must have overheard my mother's instructions. He waited, lurking, biding his time until he could strike when we were most defenseless. His knock on the door sounded harmless, even gentle, but his intentions were anything but. His voice was calm and persuasive as he lied, telling me that my mother had sent him to watch over us.

At five years old, I didn't have the capacity to question an adult's words. In my childlike innocence and disobedience, I trusted him. I believed that the world was still a place where adults kept their promises and meant what they said. So, I opened the door, unknowingly inviting a nightmare into our home. It's a moment that would redefine the way I viewed safety and trust, a moment that would echo through the years.

I remember the moments just before it happened vividly. I had been enjoying my favorite TV show, carefree and happy. The familiar sounds and vibrant colors of the screen filled the room, capturing my full attention. Television was a joyful escape, a world of imagination where nothing could go wrong— or so I believed at that innocent age.

My siblings were in the living room, too, their attention captured by the animated scenes unfolding on the television screen. They had no idea that danger had just stepped inside, that the air had shifted, thickening with a fear I couldn't voice. The man used their safety as a weapon against me, leveraging my love for them. He threatened to hurt them if I didn't follow him. His words were a dark manipulation that made my heart pound with terror. The instinct to protect my siblings, even at that young age, was stronger than my fear for myself. So, I did what he told me, allowing him to lead me into a dark room.

The room was cold and filled with shadows. Light from the fire escape outside cast strange patterns on the walls, creating an eerie atmosphere that made the space feel even more suffocating. It was as if the darkness was alive, pressing in on me, trapping me. I remember the dread that settled in my chest, the way the world seemed to shrink around me. The man's intentions were clear, and I felt powerless, too small to fight, too afraid to scream.

The person who violated my trust did so under false pretenses. He claimed to be a friend, a trusted figure, which allowed him access to our home. That lie opened the door for what became one of the most traumatic experiences of my life. There was no context of danger or unease when he first entered; he masked his intentions well, blending into the space that was supposed to be a place of refuge.

But that peace was abruptly interrupted. What followed was a dark and painful event that I struggled to process. I didn't fully grasp the magnitude of what had happened at the time, but I knew something was terribly wrong. The confusion and betrayal left a scar that lingered for years.

For so long, I carried the weight of that experience in silence, unsure of how to make sense of it or whether anyone would understand. Shame and fear often accompany such trauma, even when the victim is entirely blameless. I questioned myself, wondering if I had somehow been responsible, but deep down I knew the truth: I had been preyed upon by someone who abused the trust they falsely gained.

I did not know my abuser. He held no title or position in my life. I never saw him before that fateful day, and I had no knowledge of any connection he might have had with my family—if there was one at all. To me, he was just a stranger, an unknown figure who appeared without warning, like a shadow that crept into my world.

I trusted him, though. I was naïve, unaware of the danger that could lurk in the most unexpected places. He was persuasive, his words smooth and convincing, and in my innocence, I let my guard down. I should have never opened the door. I should have never allowed him into my home. But I did, and that moment, that decision, would change everything.

He lied to gain access, to manipulate his way into my life. I didn't know it at the time, but deep down, he knew exactly what his intentions were. His deceitful charm was a weapon, and I was the unsuspecting target. I opened the door to him, not knowing that by doing so, I was opening the door to a nightmare I couldn't escape.

It's a terrifying thing to realize that someone you trust—someone who seemed harmless, even friendly—can have such sinister intentions. What makes it even worse is the overwhelming feeling of betrayal. I felt completely powerless, unsure of how to stop it, unsure of what to do next. I had no way of knowing that the person I had allowed into my space had come with the intent to rob me of something far more precious than my security. He stole my innocence, leaving behind scars that I may never fully heal from.

He took off my panties, and pulled down his pants. I knew nothing about sex, penetration, orgasms, or sexual pleasures. I can remember the fire escape and the moon shining. And, just before he was about to have me straddle him, I heard my grandmother's voice screaming loud, she said, *"Leah, call on the name of Jesus."* So without hesitation I screamed Jesus as loud as my little voice could scream. He then threw me onto the bed, pulled up his pants and said, *"I guess you don't want to do this?"* Now mind you, my grandmother was not in the house with us. I don't know where she was—I thought maybe milwaukee?—but she could have been anywhere. All I know is, there is no distance in prayer.

*L*ooking back, I now see how many red flags were there, how many warnings I ignored or didn't see at all. But I was young and trusting, and I was not equipped to recognize the danger. I didn't know that not everyone who smiled at me had good intentions. I didn't know that kindness could mask cruelty.

There was no one to warn me about him. No one said, *"Watch out for this man."* No one helped me see him for what he truly was. If there had been someone who had warned me, maybe I would have been able to stop it. But instead, I was left alone to face this man who was more of a predator than a person.

The events of that day remain vivid in my memory, not because I recall every detail, but because certain moments changed my life forever. Her instructions were simple: *"I'll be back soon. Don't open the door for anyone except me."* As a child, I didn't fully grasp the importance of such warnings.

Looking back now, I know my mother was trying to protect us. But as a young, trusting child, I made a mistake. When there was a knock at the door, I disobeyed her. I opened it, not knowing that this single act would alter my life.

As I sat there trying to steady my breathing, the

weight of what had nearly happened began to sink in. I was overwhelmed with a mix of emotions—fear, confusion, and guilt. Even at that young age, I questioned whether I was somehow to blame. Had I done something wrong by opening the door? Would my mother be angry with me?

When she returned home, I couldn't find the words to explain what had happened. Silence became my way of coping. Shame and fear wrapped around me tightly, making it difficult to speak out. I worried that I might be blamed for disobedience, even though I was just a child who didn't understand the dangers of the world.

The pain was unbearable, but I suppressed it, burying it under layers of anger, bitterness, and resentment. I often wondered if there was something about me that made me a target. I asked myself, *"Do I have a sign on my head flashing with neon lights that says, 'All abusers apply within'?"* I was trusting, innocent, caring, and friendly—beautiful and gifted—yet it felt as though there was a hit taken out on me, and insurmountable trauma was the bullet aimed directly at my chest.

But that day marked only the beginning. It was the first of many moments that would strip away my sense of safety and leave me grappling with a trauma I didn't know how to name. The man who invaded our home was never found, never brought to justice. He disappeared, leaving behind a shattered little girl and a family that had already seen more pain than most should endure. The aftermath of that day settled into my life like a heavy fog, affecting the way I moved through the world, the way I trusted—or rather, didn't trust—people around me.

Her pain, much like mine, became a secret she carried deep within, a burden that shaped the rest of her life. She, too, had no one to shield her, no one to fight the darkness for her. The generational curse of abuse that had wrapped itself around our family continued, affecting both of us in ways we struggled to understand.

I know now that healing is a long journey, and it's one that I will continue on for the rest of my life. I also know that I can't change what happened, no matter how hard I try. But I refuse to let it define me. I refuse to let this man's actions control my future. I will find a way to move forward, to reclaim my sense of self, to restore the parts of me that he tried to steal.

Though I may never fully understand how this man wormed his way into my life, I now know that it was not my fault. I am not to blame for his evil. I was simply a person caught in the wrong place at the wrong time, too innocent to see the truth about him.

And maybe, in time, I will forgive myself for

trusting him. But for now, I will learn to trust again—slowly, cautiously, but with the knowledge that I am stronger than I ever realized. And I will never allow anyone to take my innocence again.

The abuse continued because I was afraid to speak out. The shame and confusion paralyzed me, and in some cases, there were direct threats or subtle manipulations that kept me silent. Even when there were no threats, the emotional weight of what happened made it seem impossible to tell anyone. I carried this burden alone for years, trying to navigate life while feeling broken and misunderstood. The fear and pain shaped my interactions with others, creating walls I thought would protect me but only isolated me further.

The impact of ongoing abuse was devastating. My emotional state was a tangled mess of fear, confusion, and self-doubt. I questioned my worth and often blamed myself for what had happened. Trusting others became nearly impossible, and I carried a deep sense of shame that lingered like a dark cloud over my life. Each instance of abuse compounded the previous pain, creating a seemingly endless cycle of trauma and heartbreak.

The day I tried to tell my grandmother about what happened to me in Stamford, I thought I was finally going to get the validation I needed. I trusted her with my heart—she was the one person who had always been there, or so I thought. I had carried this memory with me for so long, trying to make sense of it. I was just a child, longing for some explanation, some comfort.

But when I finally found the courage to speak up, to share the pain I had buried so deep within, her response was not what I expected. She told me I was lying. She said that it never happened. The very person I trusted more than anyone rejected me at that moment. I felt my world crumble, and that memory was buried even deeper than before. I couldn't understand why she wouldn't believe me. My grandmother, the one person I thought would understand, had turned her back on me. That rejection felt like the final blow to my already fractured spirit.

In the aftermath of that moment, I felt like I was carrying a burden too heavy to bear. I was alone with my pain. The silence that followed that rejection was suffocating. I had hoped that by speaking my truth, I would be able to make sense of it, to understand why such things happened to me. Instead, I was forced to suppress it, to hide it away like it didn't matter. My grandmother's words echoed in my mind for years. *"You're lying. It never happened."* Those words were the foundation of a belief I carried for far too long—

that my truth didn't matter, that I didn't matter. I tried to move on, to live my life, but that suppressed memory clung to me. It was always there, like an open wound I couldn't heal because no one would acknowledge it. The loneliness of carrying that secret was unbearable. No one understood the depth of my pain. I felt invisible, isolated, and unimportant. The rejection wasn't just from my grandmother; it was from the world I lived in, and I felt it in every part of me.

Looking back, I can see that my experience with my grandmother was just a small part of a much larger pattern. From a young age, I experienced abandonment and rejection in ways that no child should. My mother wasn't around the way I would have liked her to be. She was physically present, but emotionally absent. I often found myself seeking attention and affection, but it was like I was invisible. The love I craved never came, and I began to internalize the belief that I wasn't worth loving. I remember times when I felt like I was alone in the world, even though I was surrounded by people. It was as though no one could see me, no one could hear me, and certainly, no one truly cared. Those feelings of loneliness were ingrained in me from the very beginning, and they set the stage for the rest of my life.

As I entered young adulthood, the pattern of rejection and abandonment continued. But now, the emotional wounds of my childhood became entangled with the scars of abuse. I found myself in relationships that mirrored the dysfunction I had grown up with. The cycle continued, and I began to accept the abuse as my reality. The pain I experienced was all I knew. It was like I was bound to it, trapped in a never-ending loop. My sense of self-worth was non existent. The people I trusted took advantage of me, and I allowed it because I didn't know any other way. The relationships I found myself in were toxic, abusive, and emotionally draining. But even when I recognized the patterns, I couldn't break free. I believed that this was the life I was meant to live, that I was somehow destined to suffer. I had internalized the lies that had been spoken to me for so long. I was unworthy of love, unworthy of respect, and unworthy of peace. This belief became the lens through which I saw the world.

For years, I wandered through life trying to understand why all of this was happening to me. I couldn't make sense of it. Why did I experience such pain? Why was my world so full of rejection and abandonment? It felt as though I was always searching for something—a reason, a purpose, something that would explain the turmoil I was living in. But no matter how hard I searched, the answers eluded me. I felt broken inside, as though my heart and soul had been shattered into a million pieces. The more I tried to make sense of it, the more lost I became. There were moments when I thought I would never heal, when I felt like the weight of the past would crush me. But deep inside, I knew there had to be more to life than this. I had to believe there was a way out of the pain.

I remember the exact moment when everything began to change. It was a quiet moment, one that felt like the turning point in my journey. I was at my lowest, feeling like there was nowhere else to turn. In my brokenness, I turned to God. I didn't know what else to do, but I knew that I needed His healing. It wasn't an instant transformation, but I began to feel something shift within me. It was a whisper of hope, a glimmer of light in the midst of my darkness. God was reaching out to me, showing me that healing was possible. Slowly but surely, I began to understand that my worth didn't come from the people around me or the pain I had endured. My worth came from Him. I began to let go of the lies I had been carrying for so long and started to embrace the truth that God had always seen me as valuable, as loved, and as whole. The healing process was not quick or easy, but it was real, and I began to feel a sense of peace that I had never known before.

As I continued to seek God, I began to experience deliverance in a way that was both profound and life-changing. The trauma I had been carrying for so long was slowly being lifted from my heart. I could feel the chains breaking, one by one. The lies that had kept me bound no longer had a hold on me. I began to forgive those who had hurt me, including my grandmother, who had rejected me when I needed her the most. Forgiveness didn't come easily, but I knew it was necessary for my healing. I had to let go of the anger and resentment that had been holding me hostage for so long. As I forgave, I felt a weight lift off my shoulders. It was like I was no longer chained to the past. I was free to move forward, to live a life without the burden of trauma and pain.

Despite the weight of my experiences, I found a sliver of strength that helped me survive. Even when I felt crushed by the emotional toll, there was a part of me that refused to give up. The ongoing abuse left me feeling as though I had lost control over my life, but I began to understand that silence only allowed the trauma to fester. Recognizing this truth was the first step toward reclaiming my voice and beginning the healing process.

For years, the memory lingered, casting a shadow over my sense of security. I grappled with feelings of fear and mistrust, unsure of how to navigate a world that suddenly seemed much darker. But over time, I came to understand that none of it was my fault. The responsibility lay entirely with the man who sought to harm me. He was the one who crossed boundaries—not me.

*O*ur stories are different yet painfully similar. My mother had been a teenager when her innocence was stolen, and I was a mere child. She had been violated by people she didn't know, strangers who left her wounded and forever changed. I, too, was harmed by someone I didn't really know, but the impact of that moment was no less devastating. The generational trauma we experienced connected us in a way that I wouldn't fully understand until I was much older.

As I grew, I began to see my mother in a new light. The pain she carried was evident, even when she tried to hide it. Her decisions, her fears, and her struggles all made sense when viewed through the lens of her trauma. She had done the best she could, trying to love us fiercely and protect us in whatever way she knew how. But her own brokenness made it difficult for her to shield us from a world that had already hurt her so deeply. I realized that her silence about her trauma wasn't a sign of weakness but a reflection of the depth of her wounds.

Healing was a long and complicated journey. I found solace in faith, drawing strength from the same name I had called out that day. Prayer, counseling, and the support of trusted individuals became vital tools in my recovery. Slowly but surely, I began to reclaim my voice and rebuild my confidence.

One of the most important lessons I learned was that speaking out is a form of empowerment. Silence had been a prison, but sharing my story became a key to freedom. By acknowledging what happened and refusing to let it define me, I began to heal.

Today, I share my story not from a place of victimhood but from one of strength and perseverance. My hope is that others who have faced similar experiences will find courage in knowing they are not alone. Healing is possible, and reclaiming your voice is one of the most powerful steps you can take. There is hope, there is healing, and there is always the possibility of reclaiming your power.

Chapter 9

Healing

At 15 years old, I attempted suicide. I felt so unwanted, unloved, and like my life had no real meaning. The feelings of abandonment weighed heavily on me, and I struggled with low self-esteem and a lack of self-love. I was rebellious, disobedient, and surrounded by the wrong crowd—people who didn't offer love but jealousy. I didn't have the support I needed.

In a moment of overwhelming pain, I took five quaaludes and drank some gin, hoping to escape my reality. I slipped into a drug-induced coma for two days. At one point, they were about to roll my body in a rug and dispose of me in the wash. But just in the nick of time, God intervened. He woke me up.

God spoke to me and told me He spared my life. He reminded me that if I had died, I wasn't ready to meet Him. God told me if I had died I was on my way to hell. I would have been lost for all eternity. That moment of clarity, that moment of divine intervention, changed my life forever.

At that moment, when I woke up and heard God speak to me, it was as if everything in my life was brought into sharp focus. It wasn't just about surviving that night—it was about divine intervention. God, in His mercy, had spared my life for a reason. In the darkest, most hopeless moment of my existence, He revealed to me the reality of eternity, showing me that I was not ready to face Him. The weight of those words shook me to my core.

I realized that if I had died that night, I would have missed out on the life He had planned for me, a life full of purpose, love, and meaning. His grace and mercy were undeniable, and it was clear that He had given me a second chance., I knew that I had been saved for something greater. It wasn't just about being alive; it was about being alive with purpose.

That moment marked a turning point. No longer did I feel like my life was meaningless. I began to understand that even though I felt unwanted, unloved, and abandoned by the world around me, God still saw me, loved me, and had a plan for me. I didn't have to keep trying to fill the emptiness with things that didn't give me life. I started seeking Him more—asking questions, yearning for answers, and slowly letting go of the shame and guilt that had haunted me for years.

The rebellion and disobedience that I had carried with me began to fall away as I realized that my true worth came from God, not from the approval of others. My self-esteem started to shift as I understood that I was chosen, loved, and worthy of so much more than I had given myself credit for.

That moment wasn't just about physical survival; it was about spiritual awakening. God saved me for a reason, and I was determined to honor that gift of life. I had been lost, but he found me. And from that point on, I knew I would never be the same. I had been given a new lease on life, a new perspective on who I was, and a new understanding of the depth of God's love and grace.

"Before I formed thee in the belly I knew thee; and before thou camest forth out of the womb I sanctified thee, and I ordained thee a prophet unto the nations."

Jeremiah 1:5 (KJV)

From a young age, I struggled with feeling alone. I often wondered if I truly mattered, if anyone saw me, or if my presence in this world made a difference. The people I expected to lean on weren't always there, leaving me searching for love and validation in places that could never fill the void.

For years, this shaped how I viewed myself, making me believe I needed others' approval to feel worthy. But over time, I realized my strength had always been within me. I learned that I didn't need anyone else to tell me I was valuable—I had to claim it for myself. That shift in mindset freed me, reminding me that no matter who walked in or out of my life, I was enough.

Another difficult experience was witnessing the struggles of people I cared about. Seeing them change, lose themselves, and make painful choices left me feeling powerless. At first, I carried the burden as if it were my own, wondering if I could have done something to change their path.

Over time, I learned a crucial lesson: I can love someone deeply, but I cannot fight their battles for them. Their choices belong to them alone. What I can do is support, encourage, and pray—but I must also protect my own peace. Setting boundaries allowed me to care without letting their struggles consume me.

In the midst of hardship, certain moments stand

out as beacons of hope. One of my fondest memories is spending a summer day with my grandmother. In her presence, I felt safe, understood, and valued.

That day, she reminded me that life was about more than just surviving—it was about believing in something greater, about knowing that tough times don't define us. Her words gave me a renewed sense of purpose. That moment stays with me as a reminder that even in the darkest seasons, there is always a light to hold onto.

As I grew older, I encountered another challenge—feeling like my pain didn't matter. Whenever I tried to speak up, I was told to push past it, to leave the past behind. The more I suppressed my truth, the heavier it became.

The impact of the abuse was profound and long-lasting. It affected my relationships, my sense of self-worth, and my ability to trust others. However, through faith, counseling, and the support of trusted individuals, I began the journey toward healing. Speaking out, even when it was difficult, became a powerful tool for breaking the cycle of pain and shame. Though my journey has been challenging, I have learned that healing is possible. The past does not define who I am today. I am stronger, more resilient, and determined to use my voice to advocate for those who have yet to find theirs. The scars I carry are a testament to my survival, and my story is one of overcoming darkness to find light and hope once again.

This story is a testament to the fact that healing is not a straight path, but with time and support, it is possible to reclaim joy, peace, and purpose.

Today, I walk in the freedom that only God can provide. The brokenness I once felt is no longer my reality. I am healed. I am whole. The cycle of abuse and rejection that once defined my life has been broken, and I stand tall in the strength and peace that God has given me. I no longer live in the shadow of my past. I have learned to embrace who I am, flaws and all, and to love myself the way God loves me. I no longer need the validation of others to know my worth. I know that I am precious in God's eyes, and that's all that matters. The pain I once carried has been transformed into strength, and I now use my story to help others who are walking through similar struggles. God has healed me, and I am living proof that no matter how broken we may feel, there is always hope for restoration.

Looking back, I am filled with gratitude for everything I have overcome. The trauma, the pain, the rejection—it all led me to a place of healing and restoration. I am no longer defined by my past, but by the grace of God. He has given me the strength to rise above the darkness and walk in the light. I am no longer broken inside; I am whole. And for that, I will forever be thankful.

But the turning point came when I decided to own my story. I refused to stay silent about what shaped me. Speaking up was the key to my healing. I now understand that my voice carries power—not just for myself, but for others who have felt unheard. Everyone's story matters, and no one has the right to silence it.

Losing those deeply cared about was one of the hardest things I have ever faced. The pain, the grief, and the unanswered questions left me feeling shattered.

Through this, I learned the importance of making every moment count. I no longer assume people know how I feel—I tell them. I make time for the ones I love. Life is fragile, and this experience taught me to hold on to what truly matters.

My early years were filled with instability, but instead of letting it define me, I let it refine me. The uncertainties, the changes, and the hardships could have held me back, but instead, they made me adaptable and determined.

I realized that while I couldn't control my past, I could shape my future. I made the decision to rise above, to create a life rooted in strength, resilience, and purpose. Every obstacle I faced became a stepping stone toward the person I was meant to become.

Chapter 5

Taken

A man lived down the street from us on West La Loma in Rancho Cordova, California. His house was at the end of the street, a corner house that became a familiar destination for me. I would sneak over there and spend intimate moments with him, wrapped in the warmth of his presence, lost in the attention he gave me.

We never used condoms, and I was not on birth control. At the time, I didn't think much about the consequences. I was young, naive, and caught up in the feelings that being with him brought me. I can't say that he was my boyfriend because we never officially labeled our relationship. We never solidified that commitment, but what we shared felt deep. It was a connection that didn't need words—it was just there, present in every moment we spent together. I couldn't wait for his BMW to drive up West La Loma to the apartments where I lived to pick me up, and soak me in his affections.

He was older than me. I lied about my age to him, and he believed me. He was an established man who worked for Amway and had a level of stability that I found intriguing. I trusted him in a way that my young heart didn't fully understand. I craved love, attention, and affection, and he gave that to me in ways that made me feel special, wanted, and cared for.

Some of my best moments were spent with him. He would cook for me, making meals that felt like small acts of love. He showered me with the attention I had longed for, filling the emptiness that I hadn't even realized was there. Our time together was intense, passionate, and meaningful in ways that went beyond just the physical. He made me feel seen, heard, and valued, even if we never put a name to what we had.

But with passion comes consequence, and one of those consequences was my pregnancy. I don't think either of us had truly considered what could happen. We had been living in the moment, consumed by our connection, and never stopped to think about where it could lead. When I found out I was pregnant, I knew everything had changed. I was no longer just a young girl sneaking off to be with someone who made her feel special—I was now carrying a life inside me, a life that would depend on me for everything. I was excited, and afraid all at the same time, my emotions were all over the place.

*F*inding out I was pregnant was an experience that I will never forget. I was young and knew that this was going to be a life-altering moment. My mother and I had never had the 'birds and the bees' conversation. It was a topic that was never discussed in our household, and I was never put on birth control.

I did not find out through a doctor's appointment or an at-home pregnancy test. Instead, I went to Planned Parenthood to get tested. I had missed my period and could feel my body changing in ways that I had never felt before. Though I had never been pregnant before, something inside me just knew that something wasn't quite right. It was an intuition, a gut feeling that told me my life was about to change forever.

As I sat in the waiting room of Planned Parenthood, my mind was racing. I had so many thoughts running through my head. I was scared, anxious, and uncertain about what was to come. At the same time, a part of me already knew what the results were going to be. When the nurse finally came in and told me that I was pregnant, a flood of emotions washed over me. My heart pounded in my chest, my hands became clammy, and my mind seemed to go blank for a moment.

There were so many emotions fighting for dominance inside me—fear, excitement, anxiety, hope, and uncertainty. The thought of becoming a mother at such a young age was overwhelming. How was I going to take care of a baby? How was I going to tell my mother? What would her reaction be? Would she be angry? Disappointed? Supportive? So many questions filled my mind, and I had no answers.

Finding out I was pregnant was one of the most overwhelming experiences of my life. I was just a teenager, and the moment I saw the positive result, everything seemed to stand still. My heart raced, my mind was a blur, and I felt a mix of emotions that I couldn't fully understand at the time. It wasn't just one feeling that overwhelmed me; it was a combination of fear, excitement, uncertainty, and even guilt. There was a flood of thoughts running through my mind— thoughts about what the future held, how my life was about to change, and what this meant for me, for my family, and for the person I was carrying.

The first thing I felt was fear. Fear of the unknown. I was still so young, and the idea of becoming a mother at that age was both daunting and terrifying. I had always imagined my life unfolding in a certain way, but this wasn't how I had planned it. I didn't know what to expect. I didn't know how I was supposed to feel or act. I didn't have any idea how to raise a child, especially at a time when I was still trying to figure out who I was. The reality of the situation hit me hard: my life was going to be different now, and I had no idea how to navigate this new reality.

It wasn't just about being pregnant; it was about becoming a mother. That word carried so much weight. Motherhood is something people often speak of with such reverence, and yet here I was, feeling completely unprepared. The fear of not being good enough, of not having the skills or maturity to be the kind of mother I wanted to be, was overwhelming. I was scared of making mistakes, of not being able to provide the right environment for my child, and of the huge responsibility that was suddenly on my shoulders. *What if I wasn't strong enough? What if I failed?*

At the same time, however, there was this undeniable sense of excitement that also took hold of me. Amid the fear, I couldn't ignore the spark of something else—a flicker of joy at the thought of this little life growing inside me. There was something incredible about it, even though I had no idea what being pregnant truly meant. I was excited at the thought of becoming a mother, even though I was scared. I felt a deep connection to the child that was growing within me, and I couldn't help but think about what they would be like. Would they have my eyes? Would they look like the father? Would they be strong and brave, or would they be gentle and kind? There was a sense of wonder that filled my heart every time I thought about the baby.

But then came the uncertainty—the overwhelming feeling that I didn't know what was next. I had no idea how my life would unfold now. Would I be able to continue with school? How would I manage the physical and emotional tolls of pregnancy? How would I tell my family? How would I tell him? Would they be happy, disappointed, or even angry? I was unsure how the news would be received. It was a time of tremendous change, and nothing about the future seemed clear. I was faced with so many questions, and it was hard to know where to start.

What really weighed heavily on my mind was how others would perceive me. I was a teenager, pregnant, and suddenly the world felt like it was looking at me through a different lens. I feared judgment from my family, friends, and even strangers. Would they see me as irresponsible? Would they judge me for becoming pregnant so young? I had no idea how the people I cared about would react. I was already struggling with my own self-doubt, and I didn't know if I could handle the added pressure of being looked at with disappointment or disapproval. The thought of being criticized, of feeling like a failure in the eyes of others, was difficult to bear.

Despite all of these fears, there was also a strange sense of excitement deep within me. Even though I was young and not necessarily prepared for motherhood, I couldn't help but feel an odd sense of happiness. I was finally going to have someone to love and someone who would love me in return. That thought gave me a bit of comfort in the midst of all the chaos I was feeling inside. The idea of carrying life inside me, of nurturing and bringing a baby into the world, was both terrifying and beautiful.

*L*ooking back, I see now that my desire for love and connection led me into a situation that I wasn't fully prepared for. I trusted him, but I was still just a teenager, navigating feelings and emotions that were far bigger than I understood at the time.

There was no way to go back and undo what had happened. The only thing I could do was move forward, face the reality of my pregnancy, and figure out how to navigate this new chapter of my life. And as overwhelming as it was, I knew that I had to be strong—for myself, for my baby, and for the future that lay ahead.

But even in the midst of all this fear and

uncertainty, there was hope. A small, quiet voice inside me reminded me that this was a blessing, that this child, no matter how unexpected, was a gift. There was a sense of peace that came with the realization that I was carrying life. It was a reminder that this was a miracle, and though I may not have been ready for it, I would learn and grow as a mother, just as many women before me had done. In spite of all the unknowns, I knew I had the capacity for love and growth. I knew that I would do everything I could to be the best mother I could be, even if I didn't have all the answers. The idea of nurturing and caring for my child gave me hope for the future, even if the road ahead seemed long and uncertain.

There was also an undeniable sense of wonder in knowing that I was going to bring a new life into the world. That knowledge was enough to shift my perspective. Despite all the fear and uncertainty, I couldn't ignore the feeling that I was about to experience something that was bigger than myself. I was about to embark on a journey that would teach me so much about life, love, and sacrifice. There was beauty in the idea of becoming a mother, and that beauty outweighed the fear. As much as I didn't know what I was doing, I also felt a deep connection to my unborn child—a connection that only deepened as I thought about the future.

In that moment, I realized something profound. It wasn't that I was afraid of being pregnant; it was that I was afraid of not knowing how to handle everything that came with it. It wasn't just about being pregnant; it was about becoming a mother, about the responsibility and the challenges that lay ahead. But even so, the thought of holding my baby in my arms one day, of experiencing that love and bond, was enough to make me feel hopeful. Even though I didn't have all the answers, I knew that I had the desire to do my best, to love my child with everything I had.

As time went on, I began to feel more confident. The initial shock of the news began to wear off, and I started to think more practically about what being pregnant meant. I started to focus on the little things—the things I could control—and I felt a sense of strength rise within me. I began to see the beauty in the process, in the anticipation of the new life that was growing inside me. The fear was still there, but it was accompanied by a growing sense of empowerment. I was going to be a mother, and I was going to figure it out, step by step.

Looking back, I realize that those early feelings of fear, excitement, uncertainty, and hope were all part of the journey. They were all part of what it meant to become a mother. There was no manual, no set of instructions on how to handle pregnancy, but there was love. There was the realization that, despite my fear, I had within me the strength to face whatever came my way. Becoming pregnant was a moment of profound change, and it was filled with a mixture of emotions that were all necessary for the journey ahead. I may not have known what the future held, but I knew that I was ready to embrace it with all the love, fear, excitement, and hope that I could muster.

*F*inding out that I was pregnant was not only a shock to me, but it was an even bigger shock to my mother. I dreaded the moment I would have to tell her. I kept playing different scenarios in my head, trying to prepare myself for how she might react. Would she yell? Would she cry? Would she kick me out? I had no idea.

The moment my mother insisted on the abortion still echoes in my mind, a moment frozen in time that I'll never forget. It wasn't just a passing suggestion—it was a forceful decision that altered the course of my life, one that left me broken, confused, and filled with an overwhelming sense of loss. By the time she voiced her demand, I wasn't just finding out I was pregnant—I was deep into my pregnancy. My belly had already grown, and I could feel the little one kicking inside me. That connection, that bond, was already established. This wasn't just a potential life—it was a real, living being, and I loved it.

At the time, I had thought my mother would be there to help me navigate this overwhelming situation. I believed that she would offer guidance, comfort, and maybe even share some of the wisdom that only a mother could give. Instead, her words hit me like a cold slap. She told me I was too young, too unprepared. She said that raising a child wasn't something I could handle, that my life, as a teenager, wasn't ready to change in this way. What broke me more than her reasoning, however, was the harshness in her voice— her unwillingness to even consider the possibility of keeping the baby. And above all, her determination that she wouldn't help me raise my child.

It wasn't just a suggestion—it was an ultimatum. The abortion wasn't a mere idea to her; it was the only way. And in that moment, I felt a rush of conflicting emotions I couldn't even begin to understand: anger, sadness, fear, and an overwhelming sense of betrayal. My baby was moving inside of me, and yet my mother was telling me that ending that life was the only path forward. How could she not understand? How could she not see the love I already had for my baby?

But as much as my heart was screaming to protect my child, I found myself overwhelmed by her forceful will. The more she spoke, the more it felt like I was drowning. She told me that my life would be ruined, that I was too young to raise a child, that I had no way of making it work.

And with every word, I felt smaller.

I couldn't understand why she couldn't see what I saw—the baby inside me wasn't just an obstacle; it was my future, my hope, my child. But to her, all she saw was the hardship, the judgment, the struggle. My pregnancy was just a burden she couldn't bear.

I remember thinking, *Why is this my only option? Why is this the only thing she sees?*

The idea of ending my pregnancy was so foreign to me, so wrong. I had felt my baby kick, I had felt the connection, and the thought of ending that life filled me with terror. But what could I do? How could I fight her when the pressure was so intense?

The worst part of it all was that I felt like I had no voice. I was a teenager, unsure of myself, and scared out of my mind. But I loved my baby. I wanted to keep it. I wanted to raise it, no matter how difficult the journey might be. I wanted to protect that tiny life that was already a part of me. Yet, no matter how much I protested, no matter how much I tried to explain, my mother wasn't willing to listen. She kept telling me that I was too young, too immature, that I would ruin my future. It was as though my feelings didn't matter— only her opinion, her determination to make the decision for me, mattered. It was seven months past the time you are legally able to have an abortion, I call the abortion I was forced to have a back alley massacre.

The more she pushed, the more I found myself questioning everything. *Was I truly too young? Was I capable of raising a child? Would the world judge me?* My mind became a whirlwind of questions that I couldn't answer. Despite my belief that I wanted to keep my baby, the constant pressure from my mother had me second-guessing everything. The more she insisted, the more helpless I felt. I wasn't strong enough to stand up to her. She was my mother—the person I had grown to trust, the person whose opinion mattered most. And now, it felt like she was pulling me away from everything I held dear.

I couldn't bear the weight of the argument anymore. I couldn't bear the idea of standing up to my mother and fighting for what I believed in. So, I allowed myself to be coerced. The emotional weight of it was unbearable. I knew what I was doing wasn't what I wanted, but at that moment, I felt I had no other choice. I gave in, and I let her decide for me. The decision I made that day haunts me to this day. It is something that I will carry with me forever, and no matter how much time passes, I will never forget the pain of that moment.

Thirty-six seaweed sticks later, and a forced labor, and hemorrhaging, I returned to the clinic and my baby was slaughtered in my womb. And when I woke up, they said, "It's all over. Here's some cookies and juice."

The procedure itself is still a vivid memory. The physical pain wasn't what stayed with me—it was the emotional devastation. I had been forced to do something I didn't believe in, something I never wanted to do, and the guilt weighed on me. The grief was overwhelming, and I found myself questioning everything about who I was, what I stood for, and why I allowed myself to be pushed into such a decision. I felt like I had lost a part of myself, a part of my soul.

Afterward, the sadness lingered. The loss wasn't just physical—it was emotional, spiritual, and psychological. The connection I had with my baby was broken, and there was nothing I could do to fix it. I felt completely alone. My mother, the person I had trusted the most, had taken away my right to choose for myself, and I was left with the consequences of her actions.

It wasn't just a loss of a child—it was a loss of

trust, a loss of faith in my ability to make decisions for my life.

In the days and months that followed, I began to question my relationship with my mother. *How could she have done this to me? How could she have pushed me into making a decision that went against everything I believed in?* The mother I had always relied on, the one who was supposed to support me, had instead caused me unimaginable pain. And for a long time, I didn't know how to reconcile that.

But through time, healing began to take place. And, much prayer, and me crying out to the almighty God.

Our relationship didn't remain broken. Over the years, God worked in both of our hearts. I spent time in prayer, reflecting on what had happened, and slowly, I began to understand. My mother wasn't perfect—she had made mistakes, but so had I. And through God's grace, I was able to forgive her. It wasn't easy. It didn't happen overnight. But with time, our relationship began to heal. And, I had to forgive myself, and accept wholeheartedly the forgiveness of my father who loved me unconditionally.

We had tough conversations, moments of crying, moments of anger, but through it all, we both learned. We learned to communicate better, to understand each other's pain, and most importantly, we learned to forgive. God's healing power restored our relationship in ways I never thought possible. We've grown closer, and what was once a painful memory is now a chapter of healing and redemption in our lives.

Today, my relationship with my mother is stronger than it's ever been. The pain from the past doesn't define me anymore, and it doesn't define our relationship. We've both learned, and through God's grace, we've been able to move forward. Our bond is one that I cherish, and I know that our relationship is a testament to the power of forgiveness and God's healing power.

Before I received my Honorary Doctorate in Divinity, as we stood together in the bathroom, my mother said, "Leah, forgive me for forcing you to have an abortion. I should have let you have your baby."

We both received Doctorates that day.

The memory of that painful moment is still with me, but it no longer controls my life. I know that through God's love and mercy, healing is always possible, and I am thankful for the restoration of my relationship with my mother. What seemed like an insurmountable rift between us has turned into a story of growth, understanding, and forgiveness. Our relationship is stronger now, and I know that God has worked through it all to bring about healing and reconciliation.

Going through that experience reinforced my belief that abortion is not the answer. It is not just a medical procedure—it is the loss of a life, a future, and a piece of one's own soul. I know firsthand the deep pain that comes with it, the heartbreak of knowing that a child who was once alive inside of me was taken away before they ever had a chance to live. No matter the circumstances, I firmly believe that every baby deserves to be born.

Now, as a grown woman in 2025, my stance has only become stronger. I am pro-life in every sense of the word. I do not believe abortion should happen at any stage or for any reason. Life is precious from the moment of conception, and every child deserves a chance. If I could go back in time, I would have fought harder for my baby's life. I would have stood my ground, no matter the pressure. That is why today, I stand as a voice for those who cannot speak for themselves. My experience, though painful, has given me a purpose—to advocate for life and to encourage other women to choose hope, even when the path seems difficult.

Chapter 6

Vows

When I met my first husband, I was just nineteen years old. At the time, I already had a son who was a year old, and I was pregnant with my second child, a daughter. Life wasn't exactly easy, but it was my reality, and I was just trying to navigate it the best I could. It was during one of those ordinary days when I was out with my cousin getting snacks at a 7-Eleven that I crossed paths with him.

He wasn't the tallest guy or the most muscular, but he had a medium build that made him stand out. His presence was magnetic, and from the moment we met, I knew something had shifted inside me. It was like love at first sight. There was just something about him—a warmth, a kindness—that drew me in immediately. I'd never felt that way before, but something told me this could be different. We exchanged a few words, and the connection between us felt instant and undeniable.

We talked for a little while in the store, and it felt so easy. I was with my cousin, and she could see the chemistry too. After we left, he called me later that evening, and it felt like our bond deepened with every conversation we had. We quickly became inseparable. It was strange, though, because I was young, already a mother, and about to have another child, and here he was, entering my life. But I felt no hesitation—he made me feel safe, understood, and, most importantly, loved.

Despite the unusual circumstances, he never hesitated. He wasn't scared away by the fact that I had two children, neither of them his. He accepted that part of me, and that meant the world to me. It felt like he was stepping into something big—something that most men might not have been ready for. But with him, there was no doubt in my mind that he wanted to be with me and be part of our lives.

Our relationship moved fast, but it didn't feel rushed. It felt natural. We talked about our future, and soon, the decision was made: we were getting married. We didn't have a long courtship like most people might expect. We didn't need time to figure it out because we both knew deep down that we were meant to be together. Our wedding was small, intimate—just the two of us, my son, and his brother there to support us. We got married in downtown Sacramento, a simple ceremony with no frills, no distractions. It was just us, deciding that we wanted to spend our lives together, regardless of what anyone else thought.

People had their opinions, of course. Some thought we were rushing into things, others doubted whether it would work out. But none of that mattered to us. His brother, however, was supportive from the start. He told him, *"If you want to marry her, then I am here to support you."* That meant so much to me. It felt like a solid foundation, a sign that we were not alone in this, that the people who truly mattered were backing us.

I loved him deeply, and I could feel that love from him in return. He was there for me in ways that I didn't even know I needed. He was there for my son, treating him like his own, even though we hadn't yet had children of our own at the time.. The love he showed my children was one of the most beautiful things I'd ever witnessed. He wasn't just marrying me, he was accepting my children too, and that was something that made him even more special to me.

When I reflect on our time together, I realize how much he brought to my life when I needed it the most. I was young, dealing with the struggles of being a mother and navigating the complexities of life, but he made it easier. He made me feel supported and cared for. In his arms, I felt like we could take on the world, even with all the challenges we were facing.

Despite all of the hurdles we had to face—being young, having children from a previous relationship, and all the opinions from others—his commitment never wavered. He didn't care that my children weren't his biological kids. What mattered to him was that we were a family. And that meant everything to me.

Our relationship wasn't perfect—no marriage is. But the love we had, the way we supported one another, the way he accepted me and my children, made everything else worth it. We might not have had the most traditional start, but we made it our own, and for that, I'll always be grateful.

The way we met was unexpected, and the speed at which everything progressed was out of the ordinary. But sometimes, when you find something real and true, there's no need to wait or second-guess. And with him, I found that. From that first moment in the 7-Eleven, I knew my life was going to change forever—and it did.

After we got married, we made the decision to move to Rowland Heights, California, to start a new chapter in our lives. We didn't have a place of our own at first, so we stayed with my mother and stepfather while we got settled and figured things out. It wasn't ideal, but we made it work. It didn't take long, though—within a short amount of time, we were able to secure a place of our own. It felt like a fresh start, a new beginning for us as a family.

My husband, (now ex-husband) worked hard from the very start. He got a job working on the grounds of a local business, and also found work at the liquor store just down the street. He was dedicated to providing for us, and it was clear that he wanted to build a future with me. Things seemed to be moving in the right direction, and I was filled with hope and excitement for what the future held.

In the beginning, being married to him was everything I had hoped for. We were building a life together, and I loved every moment of it. I loved the way he made me feel—protected, cherished, and loved. I felt like we were partners in everything we did, and we shared many special moments during those early days. I was learning so much from him, not just about life, but also about his Creole culture, which was something so new and beautiful to me. He taught me how to cook Creole cuisine, and through those moments in the kitchen, we bonded in ways that words couldn't fully express. Cooking together became a ritual, something that connected us on a deeper level.

But, as with many relationships, things started to change. Slowly, I began to notice subtle shifts—

changes in his behavior, in the way he interacted with me. It wasn't immediate, but over time, the cracks began to show. I started hearing things—whispers, rumors—and I couldn't shake the feeling that something wasn't right. The infidelity started. He denied it, of course, but the signs were there, and it hurt. It wasn't just the physical betrayal it was the emotional toll it took on me. I found myself questioning everything, doubting what I thought I knew about him, about us.

The mental anguish that came with the infidelity was unbearable. I couldn't ignore it, no matter how hard I tried. The trust I had in him, the foundation we had built together, was slowly crumbling, and I was powerless to stop it. What hurt the most was the way it all unfolded. The emotional abuse that came along with the infidelity—gaslighting, manipulation, and the constant denial—was a pain that I hadn't anticipated. I loved him with all my heart, and this wasn't the life I had envisioned for us. I had imagined a future full of love, laughter, and togetherness, but instead, I was left feeling lost, broken, and betrayed.

It was painful, not just because of the betrayal, but because this was the man I had wanted to spend the rest of my life with. I had made a commitment to him, and I truly believed that we could overcome anything together. But the reality was that the hurt kept piling on, and it was taking a toll on me in ways I didn't fully understand at the time. The emotional scars were deep, and no amount of love or effort seemed to heal them. I was stuck in this cycle of hopelessness and heartbreak, wanting so badly for things to go back to how they were but feeling the weight of the pain every single day.

But I also learned the depth of emotional pain, the cost of infidelity, and how fragile trust can be in a relationship.

Through it all, I tried to hold on to the person I thought he was—the man I had fallen in love with, the man I married. But over time, the reality of our situation became undeniable. The mental and emotional abuse wore me down, and I began to question my own worth, my own ability to trust. I wanted so badly for everything to work out, but the relationship became more about survival than about love.

I look back now, with the benefit of time and perspective, and realize that those years were both some of the happiest and most painful of my life. I learned a great deal about myself, about love, and about what I was willing to tolerate in a relationship. The man I married was someone I wanted to spend my life with. I had dreamed of growing old with him, of sharing a future together. But the betrayal and the emotional turmoil that followed made me realize that sometimes, love alone isn't enough. Sometimes, we have to protect ourselves from the hurt that comes with staying in a relationship that no longer serves us.

Even now, the memories of that time stay with me. There are moments when I still think about the man I once loved, the man I wanted to build a future with. And while the pain of what happened remains a part of me, so does the strength I gained from it. I will always cherish the good times, the lessons learned, and the love we once shared, but I also recognize that walking away was necessary for my own peace and growth.

When we divorced the first time, I reached my breaking point—I simply couldn't take it any longer. The connection we once shared had faded, and the ability to communicate had disappeared entirely. It was painful, heartbreaking, and almost impossible to accept. The love story that once felt so powerful, so unshakable, was now crashing down around us.

Trust had been lost, and what infiltrated our lives was so unexpected that it left me reeling. I never thought we would end up here, but somehow, we did.

I remarried my first husband, believing that love deserved a second chance—that we could rebuild what had been broken. With hope in our hearts, we renewed our vows, promising once more to love, to honor, to fight for what we had lost. I was all in, ready to mend the cracks, to hold on tighter this time, to rewrite our story with a different ending.

But even as I stood beside him, vowing to start again, I could feel something in him pulling away. A quiet restlessness. An unspoken sadness. He loved me—I never doubted that—but there was a distance in him, a part of his heart I could never quite reach. And maybe I was holding back, too, afraid to admit how desperately I wanted us to work, how much I needed him to fight with me, not against me.

We tried. God knows we tried. But love alone wasn't enough to hold us together. Our second marriage unraveled, just as the first had, despite all our good intentions.

Yet, from that love, we created something beautiful. He became a father to my two children from before, loving them as his own. And together, we brought four more precious lives into this world.

Our family was whole—until the unimaginable happened.

We lost our daughter's twin to a lung disease. Nothing prepares you for that kind of pain. Nothing makes sense when you're standing in the aftermath of losing a child. And we weren't even together when it happened. Separated, grieving apart, carrying a pain so deep it fractured whatever was left between us.

The death of my daughter's twin was unexpected, and it has left a permanent mark on my heart. Both of my daughters were born premature and faced serious health issues from the start. I became not only their mother but also their nurse and caregiver. While I had family help when needed, it was my responsibility to ensure their well-being. My daughter was born with bronchopulmonary dysplasia, a chronic disease that affects newborns, and she lived with this condition until she was sixteen months old. During this time, she was on oxygen and had to take various medications to help her breathe.

The day she died is one I will never forget. I had just left for a doctor's appointment and left her at home with my mom and other family members. I received a phone call while I was out—my daughter had stopped breathing. When my mom walked into the room, she saw her twin sister trying to save her. My daughter was quickly taken outside where neighbors attempted CPR until the medics arrived. They rushed her to Orange County Children's Hospital.

When I arrived, there were police, news anchors, and a crowd of hospital staff. It felt like an overwhelming scene—one that I wasn't prepared for.

My daughter was in a coma, and as days passed, the doctors told me they wanted me to pull the plug. But I refused. I just couldn't.

The day my daughter transitioned, there was an eerie stillness in the air. I had just left her bedside to go home, clean up, and return, but as soon as I drove into my driveway, I received a call saying that she was gone. I had to turn around immediately and go back to the hospital. My stepfather took me. The hospital didn't seem to show much remorse. They did warm her body for me, but the cruelty of it all was that they paraded her body around in a body bag for everyone to see.

Her body was the first deceased person I ever saw. It was also the first funeral I ever attended. I felt overwhelming grief. I had one twin in my arms while the other lay in her casket, waiting to be laid to rest. I felt like I had let her twin down because I hadn't brought her home. Her father never saw her alive or deceased, and that's what truly broke my heart.

Her passing changed everything. It changed me. It changed him. It changed the way we saw love, life, and each other. Grief has a way of revealing the cracks you once ignored, the unspoken words, the wounds you thought time would heal. And in the end, we couldn't find our way back.

Still, I will never regret the love we shared, the family we built, the moments of joy before the sorrow.

He was, in so many ways, the greatest love and the deepest heartbreak of my life. And though our story didn't end the way I once dreamed it would, it remains ours—imperfect, painful, beautiful. A love that was, and in some ways, always will be.

I married other individuals after my first husband, each relationship proving to be worse than the last. I was searching—desperately trying to fix what I felt I had failed at so many times before. I wanted to give myself, and especially my children, the family structure that had been missing from my own childhood. The image of a white picket fence, a mother and a father raising their children together, felt like the answer, the redemption of what I had longed for as a child.

One of those marriages gave me a son, a beautiful blessing born from a union that, in hindsight, was never meant to last. With each marriage, I learned hard lessons, often too late. I realized that I had entered into relationships not from a place of wholeness but from a place of brokenness. I was seeking healing in the arms of others when the healing had to start within me.

Through it all, I came to understand that I should have never married some of those people. The wounds I carried from my love—the husband I married twice—ran deeper than I ever acknowledged. I was trying to patch up those wounds with new commitments, hoping they would somehow erase the pain of the past. But love doesn't work that way.

What I ultimately learned was that I had to take the time to heal, to learn who I was outside of a relationship. I had to fight to regain my sense of self-worth, to understand that it was not wrapped up in a man, in a marriage, or in the idea of a "perfect" family. Marriage is more than just saying *"I do."* It requires two whole people, not two broken ones looking for the other to complete them.

In the end, my journey through love and loss taught me that true healing begins when you stop searching for someone else to fix you and instead do the work to fix yourself.

Each divorce, each annulment, shattered me a little more. With every ending, I felt the weight of abandonment and rejection pressing heavier on my heart. I couldn't escape the feeling that I was the common denominator—that somehow, I was the failure. I just didn't want to fail again. I wanted so desperately for love to work, for someone to see me as worth fighting for, the way I saw them.

I loved everything in me. I believed in them, in us, in the possibility that love could overcome the brokenness. But their love was never strong enough to believe in me the way I believed in them. Time after time, I found myself standing alone, wondering why I was never enough to make them stay. All I ever wanted was a love that wouldn't give up on me.

Chapter 7

Beloved

Raising six children as a single mother was one of the hardest things I ever had to do. It wasn't just the day-to-day responsibilities—it was the constant balancing act of emotions, exhaustion, and the weight of everything that needed to be done. A lot of mothers like to say they were both the mother and the father, but I disagree with that sentiment. I was never a father. I didn't try to be something I wasn't. I was simply a mother, and that in itself was enough. I worked overtime, doing everything I could to provide, protect, and make sure my children had everything they needed. I fought every day to make sure they felt loved and cared for.

Some days felt like a never-ending loop of tasks and responsibilities. Between school runs, meals, laundry, and everything else that comes with raising a family, it felt like there was no time left for me—no space to breathe or rest. There were days when I had to push through sheer exhaustion because I knew I had no other choice. I couldn't afford to falter, even though there were moments when all I wanted to do was break down. When you're a single/divorced mother, the weight of it all is heavy, and the only thing that keeps you going is the unwavering love you have for your children.

But even with all the effort, there were moments when I felt like I was failing. I couldn't be in several places at once, no matter how much I wanted to be. I wanted to be at every school function, every sporting event, every special moment, cheering my children on and showing them that I was always there for them. But there were times when I couldn't make it. I would have to send my apologies, or worse—just not be able to show up at all. That hurt me more than I could explain. It felt like I was letting them down, even though my heart was always with them. It was painful to realize that no matter how much I gave, no matter how hard I tried, sometimes it still didn't feel like enough. I couldn't always be there to hold their hand when they needed me, or to cheer them on when they looked out into the crowd. That guilt weighed on me, but I kept going because I knew they needed me, and I had to be strong for them.

My children mean the world to me, and they still do. I was a young mother, unprepared for the vastness of the task ahead. I didn't have the tools or the experience to handle everything that came my way. There were moments when I felt completely overwhelmed. I wasn't always sure I was doing things the right way, and I questioned myself constantly. I had so many doubts, but I had something far greater than doubt—I had determination. I was determined to give my children the best life I could, to raise them with love, values, and a sense of security. I took parenting classes, reading every book I could find, seeking advice from others, and trying my best to learn what it meant to be the best mother I could be for them.

I made mistakes. Many mistakes. And looking back, I know there were things I could have done better. I could have been more patient, more present, more consistent. But what I had to learn over time was that no one is perfect. No mother is. I had to learn how to forgive myself for the things I thought I had done wrong and remind myself that I was doing the best I could. I had to let go of the guilt that haunted me, knowing that despite my flaws and shortcomings, I stayed. I stayed when it would have been easier to walk away. I stayed when I was exhausted, when I felt like I couldn't give anymore.

A PRETTY WRECK

I fought to keep us together. Through every challenge, every setback, every tear, I fought. I didn't walk away. I didn't abandon them. I didn't give up on them, even when things were hard, even when I was at my lowest. I loved them with everything I had—heart, soul, and all. That love was unbreakable, and it was the one thing that always kept me moving forward. And when I look at them now, I realize that the fact I stayed and fought for us—despite everything—was the best gift I could have ever given them. That is what matters most. They know, without a doubt, that I loved them with all my heart and that I never gave up on them, no matter the struggles.

It's not easy being a single/divorced mother, but it's worth every sacrifice, every tear, and every sleepless night. And even when it feels like you're failing, you're not. You're doing the best you can, and that's enough. That's more than enough. I held on to the word of God:

"I can do all things through Christ which strengtheneth me."

Philippians 4:13 (KJV)

For much of my life, I was searching for love in all the wrong places. I found myself involved with and eventually marrying men who were broken and unhealed. These relationships became an arena of control, manipulation, and violence—tools they used to keep me subdued and stripped of my strength.

They were threatened by my strength, by my independence, and so they sought to silence me. They used verbal arsenols to strip me of my self-worth. They wanted me to be defined not by who I was but by their distorted definition of me.

The pain of being in relationships where I wasn't seen for who I truly was—where I was viewed only as an object to control and dominate—was unbearable. But even more so was the belief that I was somehow deserving of this treatment, that I was somehow marked for abuse. *"All abusers apply inside. Now accepting applications. Sign on the dotted line."*

The final relationship I had was the most dangerous. I almost lost my life. My husband at the time looked me in the eyes and said that something inside of him told him to take my life.

But then, something miraculous happened. He heard a voice—he heard it so clearly—that told him,

"Touch not My anointed, and do My prophet no harm."
Psalm 105:15.

At that moment, he told me that someone up there loved me. In that moment, I knew I had been saved by the grace of God, even in the darkest of circumstances. I could have lost my life, but God had a purpose for me that would not be silenced by abuse, by manipulation, or by the hands of those who sought to destroy me. The plot to destroy me began in the womb of my mother but God shielded and protected me because he chose me before the foundation of the world.

Through all the pain, I eventually realized that I had been looking for love in places that could never give me what I needed. What I truly needed was healing—healing from the abuse, healing from the lies I had accepted about myself, and healing from the belief that I was defined by the men who mistreated me.

I had to find my worth again, not in the brokenness of those around me, but in the strength and love that God had placed in me. I learned that my strength was never meant to be suppressed or dimmed. It was meant to be a light, a light that no man or force of darkness could ever put out.

"*Let your light so shine before men, that they may see your good works, and glorify your Father which is in heaven.*"

Matthew 5:16

I want to begin by acknowledging that what I experienced in a same-sex relationship was something I never planned or intended. It wasn't premeditated. It happened unexpectedly, and I recognize that my involvement in this relationship, particularly with my best friend, was not in alignment with God's will. I cannot say that I am proud of it, but I must be honest about the journey it took me on.

At the time, she was married, and while her marriage wasn't ideal either, I know better now than to insert myself into a situation that was not mine to be a part of. I acknowledge that it was selfish of me to be caught up in something that, in hindsight, was wrong. What I can say, however, is that I was deeply caught up in the love, care, and attention that was being given to me. For the first time, I felt seen, valued, and loved in a way I hadn't experienced before. I didn't view the relationship as "woman on woman" or define it in those terms. I saw it as two people who cared for each other. But in reality, I was in love with being loved.

The enemy's whispers told me that I would never have the kind of love I truly desired—a love that was pure, fulfilling, and aligned with God's will. In my moments of doubt and insecurity, I believed these lies. The lies made me feel that God would never give me a the love I longed for. The deception was powerful, but through it all, the Lord, the true Lover of my soul, was dealing with me in ways I couldn't fully understand at the time.

*S*he and I were laying in bed in Las Vegas. We had just finished being intimate and we both had fallen asleep.

I woke up out of a deep sleep. Only the bedside light was on. I saw a man in a three piece suit sitting in the chair. He leaned forward elbows on his knees.

I said, *"God, who is that?"*

God answered, *"It's Satan, here to take you to hell if you don't repent.... Leah, you can't have me and her. You must choose."*

I chose God.

*L*ooking back, I understand that while I did receive love and care in this relationship, it was not the kind of love that God intended for me. Whether this Divine protest was to homosexuality or infidelity, my intrusion into the sanctity of another's marriage, I can't know for certain. I can only know I knew this path was wrong for me. I chose the destiny He had set before me. I knew that the love I had been seeking, the love I had been longing for, was found only in Him.

The love she gave me was healing in a sense. She taught me many things about self-worth and the importance of not settling for less than what I deserved. At that time in her life, I believe I was a lifeline to her, offering some sense of relief from the draining and destructive marriage she was in. At the same time, she helped me understand that I was worthy of love that would build me up, not tear me down.

However, as much as the enemy tried to lull me into believing that this was the kind of love I deserved, the Lord was working in my heart. He was reminding me of my purpose, my destiny, and His plan for my life. I know that God did not approve of the relationship, but for the first time in my life, I felt what it was like to be loved unconditionally. Not only was she my partner, but she was also a true friend—someone who wanted to see me grow and succeed, whether we were together or not. And, she still does till this very day.

I walked away, and I don't say that with bitterness, but with gratitude. I thank her for the lessons she taught me—the genuine care and love that she showed me, the self-respect and higher standards she encouraged me to uphold, and the reminder that I was worthy of unconditional love. I walked away with the knowledge that I am worth loving. I don't define my worth by past relationships, but by what God says about me. Through this experience, I gained a deeper understanding of the love that only comes from God. A love that heals, a love that restores, a love that doesn't compromise His will for my life. Her and I are still friends today and for that gift of genuine friendship I am eternally grateful.

I am not proud of my past mistakes, but I can say with certainty that God's grace has healed me, and I have learned from my experiences. I have been forgiven and restored, and I continue to grow in my relationship with God. I have learned that the love I truly need and seek is found in Him, and that His plan for me is far greater than anything I could have imagined for myself.

"For I know the thoughts that I think toward you, saith the Lord, thoughts of peace, and not of evil, to give you an expected end."

Jeremiah 29:11 (KJV)

Chapter 8

Anointed

There was a time when I was told that I would never amount to anything. I was labeled as nothing more than a "whore" and "tramp," just like my mother. I was told that I was stupid, dumb, and would never succeed in life. These words were not just words; they were weapons designed to destroy my purpose and my destiny. I was bombarded with negativity and lies about who I was and who I could be.

But as I reflect on those words today, I realize that they were nothing more than lies. They were designed to hold me back, but they did not define me. What they didn't know was that I was built to fight for my purpose, and I would not be held captive by the curses they spoke over me. I may have dropped out of high school in the 12th grade, but I wasn't willing to let that be the end of my story. I enrolled in GED classes and, as an adult, I achieved that goal as well.

Despite the struggles, setbacks, and the uphill battle, I didn't stop. I went on to obtain my Associates degree in Criminal Administration, Bachelor's degree in Biblical Studies, graduating *Magna Cum Laude.* I didn't let the negative words and predictions from others dictate my future. I continued to pursue the calling God placed on my life, and that journey led me to an Honorary Doctorate in Divinity.

I am also a published author and a Prophet of the Most High God—a title that I wear with honor, not because of anything I've done, but because of God's grace and the process He took me through. Despite the obstacles, the brokenness, and the people who doubted me, I learned that God's plan trumps any plan that man has for you.

I've learned that God's will will always prevail, and once I surrendered to His process, that's when my success began. It wasn't about what they said I would never achieve—it was about what God had already set in motion for my life. By the grace of Almighty God, I've surpassed the words of death, defeat, and negativity that were spoken over me. I stand here today as proof that God's plan for your life is greater than any opinion or circumstance.

The woman I have become today is a direct result of the transformative power of God's love and the ministry He has entrusted me with. Looking back over my life, I can clearly see how God's hand has shaped and molded me into who I am now. Ministry and my relationship with God have provided the foundation upon which I have built my character, my identity, and my purpose. These two powerful forces have not only refined me, but they have also given me a deeper understanding of my own worth, my calling, and my potential.

Growing up in church and being exposed to ministry at a young age, I have always known that my life was meant for something greater than the struggles I faced. In the midst of turmoil, hardship, and challenges, God provided me with a purpose. He gave me a reason to rise every morning, to continue despite the obstacles, and to trust in His plan for my life. Ministry became my compass, guiding me through the darkest seasons and teaching me the importance of service, compassion, and love. It became clear to me that ministry wasn't just about preaching or teaching— it was about being the hands and feet of Jesus, serving others with humility, and sharing the message of hope, healing, and restoration.

One of the most significant ways that ministry

has shaped me is in how it has transformed my identity. There was a time when I struggled with feelings of inadequacy, self-doubt, and shame. I felt unworthy of love and often questioned my purpose. But God's love and the lessons I learned through ministry taught me that I am fearfully and wonderfully made. I learned that my worth does not come from what others say about me or from the struggles I've endured, but from who God says I am. Through ministry, I have come to embrace my true identity as a daughter of the Most High God. I no longer define myself by my past mistakes, failures, or circumstances; instead, I see myself as God sees me—redeemed, loved, and equipped for a greater purpose.

The ministry also taught me the power of perseverance. Throughout my journey, there were moments when it seemed easier to give up, to walk away, or to lose hope. Life has not been without its challenges—there have been heartbreaks, disappointments, and moments of deep pain. Yet, through it all, ministry has been a source of strength. I learned to press into God's presence, to find comfort in His Word, and to lean on the support of fellow believers. I have witnessed firsthand how God uses our trials to shape us and mold us into stronger, more compassionate individuals. The woman I am today is one who does not easily give up, but one who fights with faith, knowing that God is always with me, working everything for my good.

As I have walked through the seasons of ministry, I have come to understand the importance of grace and humility. Ministry is not about elevating oneself or seeking recognition—it is about lifting others up, empowering them, and pointing them toward Christ. I have learned that true strength lies in serving others, in showing kindness, in listening, and in offering a hand to those who are struggling. God has taught me that my greatest achievements are not measured by titles or accolades, but by the lives I have touched, the love I have shown, and the hearts I have helped to heal. This humility has become a core aspect of who I am as a woman, and it guides me in everything I do.

The Ministry has also given me the platform to discover and embrace my voice. There was a time when I was silent, afraid to speak up, and unsure of what I had to offer the world. But God called me out of that place of silence and gave me the courage to speak boldly. Through ministry, I found my voice—my voice to declare the goodness of God, to encourage others, and to share my story. I realized that my testimony has the power to impact lives, to inspire others to press on, and to show them that they too can overcome. The woman I have become is one who confidently uses her voice to declare God's truth, to encourage the broken-hearted, and to spread hope to the hopeless.

The most significant transformation I have experienced, however, is in my relationship with God. Through ministry, I have grown closer to Him. I have learned to trust Him fully, to rely on His guidance, and to surrender my own plans for His greater purpose. I have learned to recognize His voice, to discern His leading, and to be obedient to His call. This deep, intimate relationship with God has been the foundation of everything I do. It is the source of my strength, my joy, and my peace. The woman I am today is one who has a steadfast faith in God, who knows that with Him, all things are possible. I have learned that it's not about my abilities, but about His anointing and power working through me.

Being in ministry has also taught me the value of community and connection. I have learned that we are not meant to walk this journey alone. God has placed people in my life who have supported, encouraged, and prayed for me. Through their friendship and mentorship, I have grown in wisdom and understanding. I have learned that ministry is a team effort—it is about building relationships, lifting each other up, and sharing the load. The woman I have become is one who values deep, meaningful connections and who seeks to build others up in love and grace.

Today, as a woman of faith, I stand firmly rooted in my calling. I walk with confidence, knowing that God has equipped me for every good work He has prepared for me. I am no longer held captive by the lies of the enemy or the limitations others have placed on me. Through ministry and God's transforming power, I have become a woman of purpose, strength, and grace. I am a woman who knows her worth, who confidently walks in her calling, and who seeks to honor God in everything I do.

The woman I have become is a testament to God's grace, His transformative power, and His unshakable love. Ministry has not only shaped me into who I am today, but it has also given me the tools to continue growing, serving, and fulfilling the purpose He has called me to. I am a woman who is continually being refined by God, a woman who has found her voice, her purpose, and her identity in Him. And for that, I am eternally grateful.

I came to a point in my life where I had to make a conscious decision—a decision that would alter the course of my future. I was no longer going to live under the weight of the lies that others had spoken over me or the generational curses that had plagued my family. I had to choose to reject them, not just in my mind but in my heart and spirit.

*I*n Scripture, we are reminded that words have power. Proverbs 18:21 says, *"The tongue has the power of life and death, and those who love it will eat its fruit."* The words spoken over me had held weight for so long, and the generational curses that had been passed down from one generation to the next seemed to have a hold on me. But I knew in my spirit that I didn't have to accept this. I was not the lies that others had spoken over me, and I was not bound to the cycles of unbroken generational curses. I break them now in Jesus' name.

Galatians 3:13-14 tells us: *"Christ redeemed us from the curse of the law by becoming a curse for us, for it is written: 'Cursed is everyone who is hung on a tree.' He redeemed us in order that the blessing given to Abraham might come to the Gentiles through Christ Jesus, so that by faith we might receive the promise of the Spirit."* Through the finished work of Jesus Christ, I was no longer bound by the curses that had been spoken over me or inherited through my family.

I made a bold decision to reject the generational curses and word curses. Deuteronomy 30:19 declares: *"This day I call the heavens and the earth as witnesses against you that I have set before you life and death, blessings and curses. Now choose life, so that you and your children may live."* I chose life. I chose to walk in the freedom that Christ offers, understanding that I was not bound to the curses that had plagued my family. I was going to live opposite to what the world or my past said I should live like. I was going to walk in the blessings of God, not the curses.

2 Corinthians 5:17 says: *"Therefore, if anyone is in Christ, the new creation has come: The old has gone, the new is here!"* Through Christ, I became a new creation, and the old curses, the old labels, and the old patterns no longer had the power to define me. I was free, and I chose to walk in that freedom.

Isaiah 54:17 affirms: *"No weapon formed against you shall prosper, and every tongue which rises against you in judgment, you shall condemn. This is the heritage of the servants of the Lord, and their righteousness is from Me,"* says the Lord. I took this as a declaration over my life. Every negative word spoken over me, every generational curse trying to hold me back, was canceled and rendered powerless through Jesus Christ. I knew I had the authority to declare victory over these curses, and I began to speak life over my future.

As I walked through this process, I sought God for both healing and deliverance. Psalm 107:20 reminds us: *"He sent His word and healed them; He rescued them from the grave."* I needed God's healing touch over my mind, heart, and spirit. I sought Him, not just for freedom from the curses, but for healing from the wounds that allowed these lies to take root in the first place. I asked Him to renew my mind and to cleanse me from all the negativity that had been spoken over me.

John 8:36 declares: *"So if the Son sets you free, you will be free indeed."* I received that freedom through Jesus. He broke every chain and every lie that had tried to hold me back. I declared my freedom In Christ and rejected the old labels that had tried to define me.

Through my decision to reject the lies, break the generational curses, and seek God for both healing and freedom, I was no longer bound but made free in Jesus Christ. His Word became the foundation of my new identity. I chose life, I chose freedom, and I chose to walk in the truth of who I am in Christ. No longer would the curses spoken over me or passed down through generations have the power to control or define me. I was free, and I would live as a living testimony of God's power to break every chain and set His people free.

*M*inistry has had an undeniable, transformative impact on my life, one that has shaped and guided me throughout my entire journey. From a young child, growing up in the church, I was surrounded by the teachings and love of God. The church was more than just a building for me—it was a sanctuary, a place of refuge from the turmoil and chaos that often surrounded me. It provided a foundation, a solid ground to stand on when everything else seemed uncertain. It has been a constant source of strength, purpose, and spiritual grounding, especially during times in my life when I felt lost, broken, and overwhelmed.

I was raised in the church, surrounded by the love and guidance of spiritual leaders who instilled in me the values of faith, service, and worship. From the early years of my life, I had a deep sense that ministry wasn't just a vocation or a profession—it was a calling, a divine appointment from God. I can vividly remember times as a child, listening to the sermons, observing the elders of the church, and quietly feeling a stirring in my spirit that one day, I would be called to serve God in a powerful way. This sense of calling stayed with me as I grew older, and despite the many trials and challenges I faced, the ministry continued to be the source of strength and guidance I needed.

Growing up in the church, I witnessed how ministry impacted others in profound ways. I saw lives being transformed, hearts healed, and broken spirits lifted. The words preached from the pulpit were not just words—they were life-changing declarations of hope, redemption, and the goodness of God. I realized that ministry was not just about preaching, teaching, or leading—it was about being the hands and feet of

Jesus in a broken world. It was about showing the love of Christ through actions, serving others, and sharing the good news of salvation with those who needed to hear it the most. In the midst of my own personal struggles, ministry became a way for me to find purpose, direction, and healing.

There were many seasons of my life that were filled with chaos and turmoil. There were moments when it seemed as though nothing was going right, when everything was falling apart, and when I was drowning in doubt, fear, and uncertainty. But it was in those very moments that ministry gave me the strength to keep going. It was through my relationship with God and my commitment to ministry that I found the resilience to push through. When my heart was heavy with grief, sorrow, and pain, ministry provided a way for me to connect with God in a deep, meaningful way. The presence of God, felt through prayer, worship, and service, became the anchor that kept me grounded, even when my circumstances seemed overwhelming.

The Ministry also gave me purpose. It gave me a reason to wake up every day, to fight through the struggles, and to continue pushing forward despite the challenges. The realization that I had been chosen by God to serve Him in this way became my inspiration to please Him and to honor the calling on my life. The very fact that God had called me to be His vessel, to share His love, and to spread the message of hope, gave me a deep sense of responsibility and determination. I realized that ministry wasn't just a privilege—it was a responsibility. It was my calling to lead others to Christ, to be an example of His love, and to share the message of salvation with anyone who would listen.

Being chosen by God to serve in ministry is a humbling experience. It is not something that I take lightly. The weight of the calling, the responsibility to lead, and the importance of being a faithful servant are always on my heart. But despite the challenges, the sacrifices, and the obstacles that come with ministry, I have never wavered in my commitment. I know that I was created for this purpose, and I have learned to trust God through every trial and triumph.

The beauty of ministry lies not just in the opportunities it provides to serve and lead, but also in the platform it offers to share the transformative power of the gospel with the world. Through ministry, I have had the privilege of preaching, teaching, and sharing the love of Jesus Christ with so many people. I have seen lives change, hearts healed, and souls saved. There is no greater joy than to see someone's life transformed by the power of God's love. The moment someone accepts Christ into their life and begins walking in their purpose is the most rewarding and fulfilling experience I can ever imagine.

The ministry has allowed me to share the good news of Jesus Christ with people from all walks of life. Whether I am speaking to a congregation, counseling an individual, or leading a Bible study, I have the opportunity to impart the love, hope, and healing that only comes from God. The Ministry has taught me the importance of compassion, humility, and understanding. It has taught me that every person has a story, every person has struggles, and every person has a unique need for Christ's love and redemption. Ministry has deepened my understanding of the human condition, and it has given me the tools to help others find healing, restoration, and purpose in Christ.

One of the most profound aspects of ministry has been learning to walk worthy of the calling God has placed on my life. I understand now that ministry isn't just about what I do in front of people—it's about who I am behind closed doors. It's about living a life that reflects the character and love of Christ in every aspect. It's about being authentic, humble, and faithful in every area of my life, knowing that my actions and words can either draw people to Christ or push them away. I have come to realize that being chosen by God is not just about a title or position—it's about living a life that honors Him, that reflects His love, and that helps others experience His grace.

The Ministry has also provided me with a sense of community and support. Throughout my journey, I have been surrounded by men and women of faith who have prayed for me, encouraged me, and walked alongside me in my growth. The church has been my family, my support system, and my strength. It has provided a safe place where I can find encouragement, accountability, and spiritual guidance. I have learned that ministry is not something we do alone—it is a collective effort, a partnership between God and His people, working together to bring His kingdom on earth as it is in heaven.

Ministry has had an extraordinary impact on my life. It has given me strength when I was weak, purpose when I was lost, and peace in the midst of turmoil. It has allowed me to experience God's love and grace in profound ways, and it has provided me with the opportunity to share that same love with others. Ministry is not just what I do—it is who I am. It is the reason I wake up every day with a heart full of gratitude, knowing that I have been chosen by God to serve Him and to make a difference in the lives of others. It is a privilege and an honor, and I will continue to live a life that reflects the calling He has placed on me, walking worthy of His appointment, sharing the gospel, and shining His light to the world.

*J*esus is alive, reigning in glory, and seated at the Father's right hand. His power stretches over both heaven and earth, leaving no rival or equal in the spiritual realm. Every demonic spirit, every dark power, and every unseen ruler is under His command. Because we belong to Him, His victory becomes our victory. We do not fight in our own strength; we stand in the authority He has given us to resist and overcome every scheme of the enemy. This authority is not symbolic—it is real, active, and meant to be used to stop the works of darkness in their tracks.

One of the enemy's most deceptive strategies is the use of familiar spirits—demonic influences that know the patterns, weaknesses, and histories of individuals and families. These spirits attach themselves to generations, often slipping in through open doors like unrepented sin, occult involvement, or cycles of iniquity passed down. Breaking free begins with repentance—turning fully to God and shutting every door the enemy has used. From there, we must step into the authority Christ gives us, speaking directly to these spirits and ordering them to leave in His name. We do not negotiate with darkness; we evict it with the power of Jesus.

Generational curses do not break on their own—they are broken when someone takes a stand in faith. That means blessing your family with your words, refusing to repeat destructive patterns, and replacing lies with God's truth. It means filling your heart and mind with Scripture so the enemy has no place to sow deception. Some battles may require the support of a trusted minister or prayer partner, and that is a sign of wisdom, not weakness. True deliverance is more than a moment of breakthrough—it's a life of prayer, vigilance, and keeping the doors of your heart closed to anything that opposes God.

We are not called to live under harassment from the enemy. God promises that He will crush Satan under our feet, and that's not poetic language—it's a declaration of complete defeat for the powers of darkness. Picture the enemy's work being ground into nothing, unable to rise again. That is the kind of victory we walk in through Christ. No familiar spirit, no generational curse, and no demonic influence can withstand the authority of God at work in you. This is your inheritance in Jesus—to live free, walk strong, and enforce the victory that He has already won.

When Jesus read from the scroll in the synagogue, He made a bold declaration: the Spirit of the Lord had anointed Him to bring hope, healing, and freedom. He said He was sent to comfort the brokenhearted, release those held captive, open blind eyes, and lift the weight from those who were crushed by life. Then He announced that the words of prophecy were coming true right before their eyes. That same Jesus has not changed—His compassion, power, and mission are just as active now as they were then.

*I*f you've been sexually abused or assaulted—whether as a child, teenager, or adult—you need to know something vital: God sees you, He hears you, and He cares. The pain you've carried, whether silent or visible, matters deeply to Him. No matter how deep the wound, the healing touch of Jesus can reach it. The shame is not yours to bear, and the fear that has stalked you is not stronger than His love. There are countless people who have experienced His restoration after similar suffering, and you can too.

Abuse is evil in every form. The Bible does not excuse it, diminish it, or overlook it—it calls it sin. God's heart is for justice, and His word makes it clear that those who harm others will answer to Him. But for the one who was hurt, God offers restoration. What happened to you is not your identity. You are not defined by what someone else chose to do. In Christ, you are offered a new future—one free from the hold of the past.

Sometimes abuse leaves more than emotional scars; it can open doors for spiritual oppression. The enemy loves to take moments of deep pain and use them to plant lies, create fear, and keep you bound. But Jesus came to break those chains. When you invite Him into those wounded places, He not only heals your heart but also removes the enemy's grip. His truth pushes out the lies. His presence dismantles the shame. His Spirit fills the places that once felt empty and broken.

If you've been living with depression, anxiety, nightmares, addictions, or the inability to trust—these are battles you don't have to fight alone. The same Jesus who healed the sick and delivered the oppressed is ready to restore you. The process may be step-by-step, but every step with Him moves you toward freedom. You are loved without condition, seen without judgment, and invited into a life where your past does not control your future.

Life can leave deep scars, whether from trauma, loss, or personal struggles. In these moments, God does not stand distant. He draws near to those who feel crushed and provides comfort that is tangible, not abstract. Healing begins when we recognize that our brokenness is seen and understood by a loving Creator.

Jesus' life on earth was only one chapter in His eternal existence. Even before His birth, He was fully with God and shared in His divine nature. Coming to earth, He embraced humanity while never losing His divinity. This truth reminds us that God's help is not temporary or limited; it is anchored in the unchanging nature of Christ.

The cross was more than an event—it was a turning point for humanity. Jesus' suffering and death opened the way for forgiveness, peace, and healing. We are not defined by our past or by the consequences of sin in the world. Instead, we are invited to live in the reality of restoration, walking each day in the freedom He purchased.

Being transformed in Christ is not a single event but a journey. We are invited to let go of past habits, anger, and fear, and to adopt a way of life shaped by His principles. Growth happens gradually through prayer, reflection, learning, and intentional choices that mirror the love and integrity of Jesus.

Faith is sometimes most visible in our stillness. When facing challenges or opposition, we are called to trust God's timing and power. Just as those who came before us witnessed God's deliverance in impossible situations, we too can rely on His strength and provision, confident that He is at work even when we cannot see the full picture.

Even the world itself longs for renewal, and God promises a future where pain, injustice, and decay will be replaced by restoration. This promise gives purpose and direction for today. Knowing that one day all things will be made right encourages us to live with hope, seek reconciliation, and reflect God's character in our daily lives.

Accepting Jesus Christ changes everything. It isn't just about altering behavior—it transforms who we are at the deepest level. The pain, mistakes, and experiences that once defined us no longer have the final word. Instead, we are given a fresh start, with a mind, heart, and spirit renewed to pursue purpose, hope, and peace.

This transformation happens as we intentionally follow God, allowing His guidance and truth to shape our daily choices. Living this new life means making decisions from a place of spiritual strength and understanding, not from past wounds or fear.

Trauma can leave lasting marks on our self-image and confidence. Yet, in Christ, we are more than our past. Each of us is uniquely designed with specific gifts, talents, and a calling that reflects God's intention.

Understanding this empowers survivors of abuse, neglect, or other hardships to embrace their worth. They can step into life not as victims, but as people created with meaning and equipped for their own journey of service, love, and personal fulfillment.

Healing is a journey that blends spiritual growth with emotional restoration. It involves:

- *Acknowledging the past*—Naming the pain and surrendering it to God.
- *Walking in authority*—Choosing to reject fear, shame, and oppression, standing firm in God's power.
- *Renewing the mind*—Replacing lies, guilt, and trauma with God's promises and wisdom.
- *Seeking support*—Engaging mentors, prayer partners, or trusted guides to navigate the journey safely.

By taking these steps, survivors can dismantle the lingering effects of trauma and begin to experience peace, restoration, and freedom.

Healing is not the end—it is the start of a purposeful life. Survivors are called to embrace their unique roles, using their experiences to grow in empathy, courage, and resilience. Life in Christ offers hope, a sense of direction, and the strength to rise above the past.

Even in a broken world, God provides a vision for renewal. We can live fully, confident that our past does not define us, and that God is actively shaping a future filled with hope, joy, and meaning.

Epilogue

I am no longer the shattered little girl, the broken woman, or the silenced soul. I am the evidence that survival is possible, healing is real, and triumph is attainable. My wreck was never the end of my story—it was the turning point. The pain that tried to bury me became the platform God used to build me.

Yes, I was a pretty wreck—damaged, yet still divinely designed. And from every trauma, God pulled out a testimony. From every scar, He drew strength. From every loss, He revealed purpose.

If you're holding this book and see yourself in these pages, know this: You, too, can rise. You are not what happened to you. You are who God called you to be before the trauma ever touched your life. And no matter how pretty the wreck may look, your healing matters more.

A PRETTY WRECK

This is not the end. It's only the beginning of your triumph.

Now go—walk boldly, love deeply, forgive freely, and live fully.

Because you, my sister, are no longer a wreck.

You are a warrior clothed in grace, crowned in glory, and walking in victory.

About the Author

Prophetess Leah M. Kelley is a certified life coach minister, mental health advocate, and survivor of unimaginable adversity. Born of a traumatic beginning and raised in the aftermath of generational pain, she has lived through sexual assault, domestic violence, abandonment, and single motherhood—yet emerged with unshakable faith and a purpose-driven heart.

With bold transparency and prophetic insight, Prophetess Kelley uses her voice to break generational cycles, uplift the broken, and remind readers that healing is not only possible—it's promised. Through her life, ministry, and calling as a Prophetess, she has inspired countless women and men to rise from their own wreckage and step into triumph.

A Pretty Wreck: From Trauma to Triumph is more than her memoir—it's a movement. A testament that beauty can rise from brokenness, and a declaration that your past does not disqualify your future.

www.ingramcontent.com/pod-product-compliance
Lightning Source LLC
Chambersburg PA
CBHW071749120626
46550CB00002B/721